Chris Brewster is an industrial relations lecturer and consultant at the Cranfield School of Management. He acquired various insights into industrial relations through working with the AEU, the Commission on Industrial Relations and in the construction and air transport industries. He also worked at Kingston Regional Management Centre and as a consultant.

Dr Brewster is the author of *Understanding Industrial Relations* in the Pan Breakthrough series.

D1387376

PAN MANAGEMENT GUIDES

Other books in the series:

PAN MANAGEMENT GUIDES

Industrial Relations

Chris Brewster

A Pan Original
Pan Books London and Sydney

First published 1987 by Pan Books Ltd,
Cavaye Place, London SW10 9PG
9 8 7 6 5 4 3 2 1
© Chris Brewster 1987
ISBN 0 330 29365 6
Photoset by Parker Typesetting Service, Leicester
Printed and bound in Great Britain by
Collins, Glasgow

Contents

Introduction

This book is a simple, straightforward guide to industrial relations. It is written for managers in industry and commerce, in the public and private sectors, whatever the size of the organization. It assumes managerial knowledge but no industrial relations expertise on the part of readers.

1 What is 'Industrial Relations'?

Every day newspapers and news bulletins cover industrial relations, often as 'headline' stories. Yet there is no generally agreed definition of the subject, nor sufficient appreciation of its real impact.

Fact or opinion?

Everything that is said or written about industrial relations is based on a range of assumptions about fundamental issues of what is right, fair and reasonable. The values that we hold – and the muddled and contradictory form they can take – will have a major impact on our view of the subject.

There is little in industrial relations that we can confidently describe as fact. We shall find that even basic 'facts' (such as the number of trade unions) are open to dispute.

We should not be surprised, therefore, if the problems that some people raise are not accepted as problems by others; or, if they are, that the solutions proposed vary significantly.

This variety of views makes industrial relations fascinating, but frustrating. Many managers, particularly the more numerate or scientific, are happier working with exact and 'correct' answers. There are 'right' ways of solving engineering or accountancy problems. With people problems, answers must be adjusted to circumstances and individuals.

This does not mean that we cannot analyse the subject, any more than we are unable to study music. There are basic patterns, 'highs' and 'lows', and different styles. Underlying our views of these patterns and styles, however, are our own preconceptions and preferences.

Definitions

There is no 'correct' definition of the subject. Definitions usually embrace relationships between managers and trade unions, sometimes include dealing with governments but are often much wider, covering people at work and the terms and conditions under which they are employed.

Here we will define industrial relations as concerning the employment relationship between employees and managers. Either side may be represented by separate organizations: trade unions or employers' associations. The government and government agencies concerned with the workplace and employment will also frequently be involved, but the focus will be on the employment relationship.

Industrial relations can be seen as a circle with blurred edges. Clearly issues such as wage negotiations, union complaints about shift work or the introduction of new disciplinary rules will be at the centre of the circle. An employee's grievance about the positioning of his desk, or a health and safety issue, will be close to the centre. Issues such as the purchase of new equipment or a new customer service arrangement will be at the margin – but may move into the centre if they seriously affect the employees' work.

All managerial actions – financial, operational, marketing – can impinge upon industrial relations.

Work in Britain

Industrial relations is about people at work. Nearly all males and about 60 per cent of females between school-leaving and retirement ages work or want to work. In Britain this means that some twenty-four million people are at work. Over three million are unemployed.

Most people work for someone else. Less than 3 per cent own their own businesses and employ others. Only 9 per cent work for themselves, employing just their own labour.

Roughly one in ten of those who are employed work in managerial roles. They fall into both managerial and employee categories and have a particularly complicated role in industrial relations matters.

What about the self-employed, working only for themselves? History is littered with cases of self-employed people who caused industrial relations disputes. Workers at a factory might claim that a self-employed painter is putting one of the regular factory-employed painters out of work; or they might be annoyed by the extra money he is being paid for the painting contract (or by how cheaply he is expected to work). So even self-employed workers become involved in industrial relations.

Normally, however, we use the term to refer to relationships between employees and their employers or managers. To a significant extent this relationship is governed by the contract of employment.

The contract of employment

It is still the case that how much an individual is paid, what he has to do for it and the circumstances in which he works are all decided between employers or managers and employees or their representatives.

In practice, individual employees rarely have the chance to negotiate on the basic terms of the relationship between themselves and their boss. Typically wage rates, hours of work and the sort of work expected are decided by negotiation with a trade union or by the updating of historical tradition. The employee agrees merely to join the organization on those terms and conditions.

Of course, many aspects of employee-managerial relations fall outside the formal written terms of the contract of employment.

The importance of industrial relations

Industrial relations is important because:

- work is a central activity for most adults
- everyone is affected by industrial relations
- bad industrial relations can damage our economy
- good industrial relations give potential and far-reaching benefits.

Work as a central activity

Work dominates time; an individual may spend up to half a normal working day in getting ready for work, travelling there, being at work, journeying home. Most of us spend more of our waking hours at work than everywhere else put together, at least on a working day.

Work affects our social life. How much money we have to spend, whom we know, how other people regard us, how we are expected to behave – in short, how we live is determined by our work. Work will have an impact on how happy we are, what our health is like, who our friends are, where we live. So work is vital to us. That means, in turn, that industrial relations is important.

The impact of industrial relations

Suppose a major engineering factory and the nearby office of a building society both suffer from poor industrial relations. In the factory this will take the form of antagonism between union representatives and management as well as between the individual employees and managers. In the building society office it will result in strained relations between, say, counter staff and the manager.

These problems have impacts on everyone else: industrial action such as go-slows or bans on overtime working in the factory may mean that we cannot buy the goods we need. In the building society office we may find that the staff are less helpful than usual, or make mistakes in our accounts.

Nor does the workplace where industrial relations is poor have to be located near us. The factory may supply goods all over the country. It may be at the building society's head office, two hundred miles away, that an aggrieved employee fails to pay proper attention to our account.

Industrial relations affect us all in these undramatic ways. It can also have a more general and visible impact. A strike on the railways affects millions. Industrial action by teachers has an impact wherever there are schoolchildren and may have a consequent impact on many other workplaces if parents have to stay at home. A dispute in the banks will give nearly everyone problems. This widespread effect is one of the reasons why press and television pay such close attention to industrial relations issues.

Economic impact of bad industrial relations

The effect of industrial relations problems does not lie merely in individual or mass inconvenience. These problems also have a significant economic result. Bad industrial relations make organizations less able to fulfil their overall objectives.

Aggrieved employees will work less well, may refuse

certain work or may cease to work altogether by leaving that employment or going on strike. This will threaten profits or restrict the service provided. If such a situation becomes widespread, in different organizations, it will weaken the economy of the country as a whole.

There are, generally, around 2,000 strikes reported in the United Kingdom per year. In an average year, they occur in only a fraction of one per cent of establishments. Even in the manufacturing industries well over 90 per cent of workplaces have no strikes in an average year.

Country	Average for ten years 1973–82
United Kingdom	870
Australia	1290
Belgium	420
Canada	1880
Denmark	710
France	280
West Germany	60
Italy	1780
Japan	150
Netherlands	80
USA	1010

Table 1 *Working days lost per 1,000 employees through industrial disputes in OECD countries – all industries and services.*

It is worth comparing the number of days lost through strikes with the number of days lost through sickness. In the 1970s, when strikes caused more working days to be lost than at any time since the Second World War, ten million working days were lost through industrial disputes in the average year. In the same period, 350 million days were lost each year through sickness. It has consequently been suggested that a cure for the common cold would have more impact on industrial productivity than ending all strikes.

How does the United Kingdom stand compared with other countries? Table 1 shows that, in the United Kingdom during the ten years up to and including 1982, 870 days were lost per 1,000 employees due to strikes. In other words, for every 1,000 workers in employment (with each working approximately 240 days per year) a total amongst all of them of 870 days were spent on strike.

The table shows that Britain lies about middle of the league. This may surprise you – it certainly does not fit the newspaper image. The British pattern is different from others in two respects. First, 95 per cent of strikes in the United Kingdom are 'unofficial' – they are decided upon and carried out at the local level and not formally approved by the trade union's regional or national executives. (We will consider this again in the chapter on trade unions.)

Second, strikes have traditionally been concentrated in a few industries (coalmining, docks, motor vehicle manufacture, shipbuilding and iron and steel). Recently, however, this concentration has declined as those industries become less strike-prone and others take up the strike weapon.

The potential benefits of good industrial relations

Poor industrial relations are a cause of distress for those involved and a source of inconvenience for others, as well as being an economic problem for organisations and the country as a whole. Equally, good industrial relations have a positive impact; work will be more enjoyable, service or profit will be better, there will be a gain for the national economy.

Why is industrial relations good in some situations and less good in others? There is no simple answer.

The working environment (the industry, size of workplace and occupation) affects industrial relations. There is considerable evidence that certain industries have better industrial relations than others and that better industrial relations are to be found in smaller workplaces and amongst certain occupational groups.

Nevertheless, even in similar circumstances, some organizations enjoy better industrial relations than others. The obvious explanation for this lies in the way these organizations are managed. Good industrial relations can be achieved where management consciously plans to create it, integrates industrial relations into its business objectives and gives it a high priority in the operation of the organization's work.

Organizations can manage in a way which generates good industrial relations. (We will return to this point later.)

If managers want to develop good industrial relations they will need to know *who* is involved and *what* happens. Read on.

Where work occurs

Our definition of industrial relations could apply at national, industry or organizational levels. Most contact between managers and workers occurs within organizations: in factories, offices, departments, shops, sites and studios.

When we think about a workplace, the first thing we need to be clear about is who works where. Leaving aside the old joke – 'How many people work here?' 'Oh, about half of them' – we need to consider the variety of situations in which people are employed. There are four important factors to consider:

- industry or industrial sector
- whether private or public organization
- size of workplace
- occupation.

Industry or industrial sector

There has been an overall shift in the location of people's employment which we can show if we group industries into three categories:

- *primary* – by which is meant extracting a living directly from nature (mining, fishing, agriculture)
- *manufacturing* – the making of things, often in (manu) factories (engineering, chemicals, and textiles)
- *service* – the rest of employment (including public services such as education, health care and transport; an enormous range of private services such as hotels, shops, banks and washing-machine repairing).

These are only broad groupings. Manufacturing, for example, will cover everything from the making of horse harnesses to the production of microchips.

Whole industries grow and decline. There is a continuing reduction in the number of people employed in agriculture, mining, railways and steelmaking. There are more employees in computer and video manufacture. The balance between the different sectors of work is also changing. We have seen a growth in the service sector of the British economy at the expense of manufacturing.

There are important differences between manufacturing jobs and service jobs which are related to industrial relations:

- service jobs tend to be cleaner
- manufacturing is often carried out by large groups of workers, service jobs are more often done singly or in small groups
- service jobs often involve meeting members of the public, manufacturing jobs rarely do
- manufacturing is usually carried out in one

immovable location, many service jobs involve the worker moving around geographical areas.

Private vs public sector

In 1979, the Conservative government, under Margaret Thatcher, began a deliberate policy of 'rolling back' the numbers employed in the public sector. This was an attempt to reverse another trend in employment. Until recently, it was not just the case that the service industries had become comparatively bigger.

Public Sector services – those owned by the State – were employing more and more of the workforce. In broad terms, during the two decades up to 1980, it was the public service sector of employment which grew most rapidly. Significant growth areas were central government (usually referred to as the civil service) and local government, including the health service, education, local authorities, police. The reduction of employment in manufacturing and the growth in public employment had a significant impact on the way people work, and therefore on industrial relations.

Size of workplace

There are three million enterprises in Britain, ranging in size from a workforce of one to workforces employing thousands. The larger organizations are often split up over many geographical locations (they are sometimes referred to as 'multi-plant' or 'multi-site').

Take the example of Tube Investments (TI), one of Britain's major manufacturing companies. In fact TI is a group of companies making products such as heavy steel tube, Tower Kitchenware, Glowworm heating equipment and Sturmey Archer gears. Some of these companies in turn operate in several geographically spread buildings.

Most workplaces are very small. Nearly half of all employees, however, are employed in a small number of large workplaces with over 1000 employees. The range is enormous. I worked for a while with a steeplejack gang, high up in the roof of a Sheffield steelworks – a giant place, nearly half a mile long, full of awesome machinery, heat and noise. Below, dwarfed by the surroundings, hundreds of people worked. My next job was in a quiet office, working with seven others. You need to bear in mind the variety of workplace sizes throughout any consideration of industrial relations.

There has been a continual growth in size of workplaces throughout this century but that may now be reversing. First, as the recession has hit companies, they have made employees redundant. Often the bigger establishments find it easier to reduce the number of staff they employ. Second, new technological developments mean that people no longer need to work in such large conglomerations: it is now easier to organize work in smaller units, linked by sophisticated communications systems.

The occupational structure

So far we have isolated three factors; industrial sector, private or public organization, and size of workplace. The fourth factor is occupation, meaning the type of job being performed. Usually, though not always, employees are classified according to the things they are expected to do.

In Britain, unlike Japan for instance, people are not employed as a 'company worker', rather they are employed as an electrician, nurse, computer programmer, storekeeper or whatever. They are not generally expected, and do not expect themselves, to change from doing an electrician's job to a nurse's or from programming to shopkeeping. These expectations are part of the implied terms of the contract of employment – and Parliament has insisted that the occupational title is included in the written particulars of the contract that employees must be given. Ask a Japanese worker what he does and he will reply, 'I work for Mitsubishi' (or Nissan, etc.); ask a British worker what he does and he will say, 'I am a welder' (or an accountant, etc.).

This reflects traditional work patterns. In Britain employees will change jobs, maybe quite often. They will move from being a salesman in one firm to being a salesman in another, and then perhaps to being a salesman in a totally different industry. But they will stay a salesman. In Japan they will move from being a production worker to a salesman to an office worker – but all with the same company.

Occupational differences are an important facet of industrial relations and many trade unions have established an occupational link. There is one major union for engineers, one for electricians, one for airline pilots, one for musicians, one for health visitors and so on.

Changes in work

The four factors discussed are all subject to *change*. The numbers in each occupation will change; they will do so as the industries change. A smaller mining industry will mean fewer miners; a growing computer industry will mean more computer designers, computer engineers and programmers. There will also be changes associated with the introduction of new services. A greater emphasis on welfare, for example, has meant that there are now more social workers than before. There will be changes, too, in the way some occupations are carried out. Railway signalmen used to work in isolated 'boxes' up and down railway lines using muscle-power to pull heavy iron gears. Now they work in groups in well-lit offices monitoring and controlling highly sophisticated computerized signals via a complex visual display.

Underlying many changes is the introduction of new technology. The introduction of new machinery, computer-aided design and manufacture and, in particular, new information technology in the office has created whole new industries and revolutionized existing ones. These changes are continuing. They have affected industries, sectors and occupations. Sooner or later, new technologies will affect every job. Employment is enormously varied – and continually changing.

So too industrial relations is very complex – and dynamic.

2 Management

Management plays a key, some would argue, *the* key role in industrial relations. To understand that role we must understand the differences within management and the variety of ways that they can be involved, and have at least a brief acquaintance with the organizations that represent management in industrial relations.

The overall responsibility for industrial relations in Britain is shared between managers, unions and the state agencies involved. The responsibility for industrial relations within the organization is also shared – but the major responsibility rests with management. Management is responsible for running the organization and should accept responsibility for the industrial relations which are an integral part of that process.

There is a view that responsibility for bad industrial relations lies with the trade unions. Certainly, when there is an industrial dispute and strikes are called it is the unions' action which is most obvious. But even here management cannot be absolved from blame if industrial relations in the organization has reached the point where employees are prepared to stop work.

The view that management is mainly responsible for developing and maintaining industrial relations is still controversial. The decreasing power of the unions over the last few years has, however, made management's role more visible. There is also a greater acceptance among managers themselves of the impact that good management can have upon industrial relations.

Managers or owners?

Our definition of industrial relations (p.10) refers to managers and their organizations. Many other definitions of the subject are more 'logical': in opposition to employees they talk about employers and their organizations.

We will continue to refer to 'managers' here for two reasons. First, most organizations do not belong to an employer. The notion of an 'employer' or 'owner of the business' is one that is obviously useful in explaining the operation of a small business – or a large business owned by one family (such as Pilkington Glass, or Tesco or Ford).

But who 'owns' a giant multinational corporation, or a local authority, or a bank or pension fund, or the Co-operative Wholesale Society? Who is the 'employer' in such cases? In law a particular individual – often 'the company secretary' reporting to the board of directors – can be taken to represent the employer. But in practice this is an abstraction. Even the local authority's council, or the bank's board or the CWS executive committee are in reality representing the local ratepayers, or the shareholders or the members respectively. They are managing the concern on behalf of others. Since 'owners' of small companies also 'manage' their concerns, we can use the term 'manager' or 'management' to cover all those who are involved in running organizations.

The second main advantage of referring to 'managers' is that it is closer to the reality of work. It may not be easy to identify who the employer is; it is far easier to know who your boss is – and who the other managers in the organization are. The employer may be an abstraction; but the managers are real – you can bump into them, or annoy them or keep out of their way.

And their impact on you will be very apparent.

We should beware, however, of assuming that the

interests of managers and owners will be identical. There is much debate about whether a management can have different interests from the owners of the business. On one side, it is argued that ownership is now so widespread and fragmented that it is in fact the managers who control the business (or at least the senior executive managers). On the other side, it is said that owner control still exists, but is hidden, and/or that managers effectively control the business just as the owners would. This is the result of the common background which senior managers share with owners, the extent to which managers are selected because they share the same beliefs, and the way they are encouraged to identify themselves with the owners.

Managerial objectives

On average, about one tenth of an organization's employees may be classified as managerial. What is it that sets this group apart? How do managers differ from other employers?

First, managers have a different job to do. Bertrand Russell once said that there are two kinds of work: the first involves altering the position of matter at or near the surface of the earth; the second involves telling other people to do it. He argued that the key differences were that the second was pleasant and well paid, whilst the first was often neither. This was perhaps a little tongue-in-cheek. The point, however, is accurate. The key tasks of management are deciding on priorities for groups of people and controlling economic and human resources to achieve those priorities. Other employees do not make such decisions. While they may control economic resources, they do not, or only occasionally, control other people.

Second, managers generally have a different background; more education and training.

Management and industrial relations

The task of management embraces all the activities of the organization. Most managers, and most writers on management, see industrial relations, even on our wide definition, as a subordinate activity. But the key task of controlling other people, and the impact of industrial relations that we examined in Chapter 1, mean that it is an important subordinate activity.

Management involves working through other people: motivating them to do the work while the manager plans, organizes, coordinates and controls it. In all these activities most managers are trying to achieve targets: sales, budgets, production, service, time deadlines. Managerial relationships with employees and their representatives are just means to these ends.

They are, of course, crucial means. Poor industrial relations could make it impossible for management to achieve its objectives. The wages and other costs (such as national insurance and pensions) associated with employing staff are the major operating cost for most organizations. If those costs can be kept down, or the work achieved for those costs can be increased, management will be closer to achieving key objectives of profit or service.

Yet managers still tend to consider industrial relations as less important than production, sales or finance. It moves up their priority list only when there is a very obvious problem.

This low priority results from five factors.

1 Historically human labour has at most times been cheap, available and easily replaced.
2 It is only comparatively recently that many organizations have become unionized. The consequences of collective action are much more visible than individual absenteeism, staff turnover or low morale.
3 Management experience and training is often technical: concerned with the *task* that the individual comes to

manage rather than with the issue of managing people.
4 It is easier to measure production, service quality or
   marketing success than to measure industrial
   relations.
5 Blame for industrial relations problems can be passed
   on to others (shop stewards, employees, union officials) in a way that blame elsewhere cannot.

This has many important consequences; if employees
believe that only union action will raise an issue in
importance in management's eyes, that is the route they
will adopt. There is, however, pressure to change. The
factors noted above are not static. In particular,
increased international competition is forcing organizations to look more rigorously at their major operating
cost – manpower. At the same time, reduction in trade
union influence in the 1980s has made excuses which
blame union opposition seem far-fetched. Paradoxically, these two changes have combined to raise the
priority accorded to industrial relations by many managers. They have also, as we shall see in the final chapter, led managements to adopt new approaches to the
subject.

Differences within management

It is remarkable that managers within an organization
act in common as much as they do. This is so much a
part of our everyday experience that we often fail to
notice it. People will quite readily tell you that X is a
good company to work for, Y is all right but not as good
as X and you work in Z only if you are desperate. It does
not matter whether they are right or not (unless you are
offered a job in one). What is significant is that these
distinctions can be made even between apparently similar companies in the same industry. What people often
mean, and sometimes say, is that management in one

organization treats the employees well, in another not so well.

They have identified sufficient similarity of behaviour among a group of very different individuals to be able to classify them all as having a certain management style. This, among the very varied individuals (and occasionally eccentric individualists) that make up a management team, is indeed remarkable.

All human beings are individuals but it is by categorizing them as members of groups that we begin to cope with their varied characters. So we start to think of them as male or female, married or unmarried, of particular nationalities or with certain physical attributes, and in groups which indicate their relationships to other people (husband, father) or their work (doctor, bricklayer).

Managers are most often categorized on two scales: 'functional' (referring to the variations between tasks or departments) and 'hierarchical' (variations between different status levels).

Departmental differences

Most organizations divide employees according to the tasks they are expected to perform. Each group is under the direction and control of a manager. In Britain it is common for managers to come from the occupational group they are in charge of. The larger the organization, the more managers there will be in any particular occupational, or 'functional' group.

Inevitably, therefore, even in the smallest organizations, we can differentiate between managers according to the functions they are managing. Typically, there may be a production or service manager, a sales manager, an accounts manager, an administration manager; the list is endless. In the largest organizations there may be hundreds of different functional categories. We can, therefore, find numbers of managers in any one organization who have a similar standing or status but are involved in running totally different parts of the overall operation. This often gives rise to jealousies and conflict.

Sales managers, for example, can encourage their salesmen to obtain orders by allowing them to offer particular tailor-made specifications for different clients. In this way the number and value of sales are increased and the sales managers are meeting their objectives. Production managers, on the other hand, have different objectives. Their job is to ensure cheap and efficient production and to as high a standard as possible. The best way to do this is to produce large quantities of identical items. Many management meetings are spent trying to reconcile the desire of sales managers to push tailor-made items with the desire of the production managers to ensure standardization.

'Line' and 'staff' managers

Not only is there a differentiation between functions, and therefore between functional managers; a differentiation is often made between what are known as 'line' managers and what are known as 'staff' managers. Broadly, a line manager is one who is directly concerned with the organization and making of products or the provision of the service. Staff managers are those who are responsible for backing up the line manager by providing support in areas such as finance, publicity or, particularly relevant here, industrial relations. Line managers are all involved in industrial relations. When we look at industrial relations policies (in Chapter 7) we will see that they are not only involved, but are central to it. And yet many companies – especially the larger ones – employ specialist industrial relations managers.

They are not always called that. They may be called 'personnel managers', 'labour relations managers', 'staff officers', 'administration managers'. The task of these specialist managers is hotly debated and varies from organization to organization. In general, however, it is to monitor and control elements of the contract of employment and, as part of that, to handle the more important relations with trade unions.

The debate about their job centres on whether or not they should take over parts of the line managers' task. Some managers argue that the IR specialists should help line managers with advice, but leave the decisions and even the action to the line manager. They, after all, are responsible for their unit's performance. Others, often the specialists themselves, argue that if industrial relations are to be controlled, then the specialists must 'run the show'. They should make the decisions and, for example, run all meetings with the trade unions. They point to the fact that inconsistency between managers is a frequent cause of industrial relations disputes.

Levels of management

If different functions are important in management so are different levels. The 'hierarchy' of management, the way it is structured in different layers of authority, determines to a large extent each manager's task. I have worked in a small organization where everyone was responsible to the managing director. In that company our functional tasks were the only determinant in our jobs. I have also worked in organizations that employed many thousands, where some people reported to me and I reported to someone above me in the structure. Not only was I responsible to my boss for my work and my actions, I was also responsible for the work and results of the people who reported to me.

This is the typical pattern in modern organizations. Usually, as soon as an organization employs more than a handful of people, there are different levels built in.

When someone becomes responsible for someone else's work and activities, we can start speaking of them as a manager. This is when we start getting into the area of industrial relations.

Organizations may have many levels in a hierarchy. The differences between these levels affect the managers' jobs. It is not unusual for those at the lower levels of management to share a room with those they manage, even to do some of the work themselves. They are in a very good position to understand the work and the people who do it. They know how much an individual can be expected to do, how quickly they can do it, who is best at what. They know which of their staff would be prepared to work late and which need extra overtime money. The higher-level managers do not know these details. They have access to other information; how much they can afford to pay out in overtime payments within their budget, or how the amount of work required may change over the next few months.

As with functional differences, these hierarchical distinctions can create tensions between the levels. Managers at senior levels may want to reduce staff costs, for example, whereas managers at the lower levels may find it embarrassing to refuse overtime, or may realize more clearly the effect on output or service.

In general, managers at the lower levels are more aware of and concerned with the immediate work operation and the needs of individual members of staff. Managers at the higher levels are focused on the overall business requirements; they consider employees, where appropriate, as groups rather than individuals.

Departments, levels and industrial relations

These departmental and functional differences are crucial to industrial relations. Employees judge organizations largely on the basis of the way they are treated by their managers. This treatment will differ between individual managers, and it will often vary between departments. The hierarchical structure, however, means that in most organizations a management 'style' is established; managers who don't act in the required way are directed by senior management to change their behaviour. In this way the organization develops a consistency of action amongst individual managers.

Employees react to the individual behaviour of their own manager. They also react to the overall management style of the organization. Employee representatives and trade unions will be involved at both levels, as we shall see. But they too will be reacting to the behaviour of management.

Managers, and management, recur throughout this book as a key group of actors on the industrial relations stage. For now, we need to examine briefly two related matters; the organizations that represent managements in their dealings with employees and trade unions, the employers' associations; and the unique position of managers as employees in their own right.

Employers' Associations

Just as employees in many organizations join together to form trade unions, so employers in many cases join together to form employers' associations. The number of trade unions has declined over the years with amalgamation. Employers' associations have also fallen in numbers and their power and influence is declining. There are now some 400 employers' associations in the

United Kingdom, active in industrial relations. The
better known ones include the Engineering Employers'
Federation (EEF), the National Federation of Building
Trade Employers (NFBTE), the Federation of Clearing
Bank Employers, the Chemical Industries Association
(CIA), The Newspaper Publishers' Association (NPA)
and the Local Authorities Conditions of Service
Advisory Board (LACSAB).

They provide a full range of services and have per-
manent secretariats and impressive headquarters.
Others are much smaller, with members meeting only
occasionally. It is impossible to generalize and be accurate; we will consider employers' associations, under
four headings:

- membership and finance
- organizational structure
- staffing
- activities.

Membership and Finance are usually straightforward.
Most associations are open to all organizations in a
particular industry (limited by geographical region in
some cases), and aim to cover as many of them as
possible. They sometimes restrict membership to 'repu-
table businesses' and always insist that members agree
to abide by the policy of the association. In practice this
is not a very onerous requirement. The other requirement is, naturally, that members pay their subscriptions. Most employers' associations are largely funded
direct from subscription income.

Organizational structures are varied. There are two broad
types of association structure. Some associations are
single national bodies which aim to recruit all the organizations in their industry. They may be public or private
sector associations and may or may not have branches
or regional structures. Other associations recruit

regionally and have an overall body at national level to which the associations belong; this format is typified by the Engineering Employers' Federation and its constituent local associations. It is mainly found in the private manufacturing sector.

Staffing of the associations varies considerably too. Some employ a large number of full-time staff specializing in all sorts of subjects; many employ just a small administrative secretariat; and many have no full-time staff and rely on local solicitors or accountants as central figures.

Activities of employers' associations are closely related to their staffing. What do they do? Much of their work falls outside industrial relations; legal and commercial advice, for example. Many of the associations are active in industrial relations, though, either in conducting negotiations with trade unions themselves or by providing specialist advice, or both.

Several employers' associations, usually the larger ones with full-time staff, negotiate directly with trade unions, or with an equivalent federation of trade unions, to establish terms and conditions of employment for the whole industry. These will sometimes determine all the major aspects of the remuneration package and important conditions of work: the electrical contracting industry is an example. Sometimes they determine most of the key aspects, and leave others to be negotiated locally. Usually, however, they set standards for basic pay and hours of work, and member firms are free to negotiate additional sums as and when they see fit.

Specialist advice is more *ad hoc*, given in response to requests from individual companies in most cases. Sometimes, the association will issue guidance on how to cope with a new piece of legislation or a problem that is affecting several member organizations simultaneously. Very often the specialists will act as back-up to, or even in place of, a firm's personnel department – advising on disciplinary and work-related issues, payment systems or responses to trade union demands. Often too the employers' association will be involved, with officials from the unions, in adjudicating on disputes that cannot be handled within the member organization.

Employers' associations have declined in membership and importance since the Second World War. The main reason is the decline of national industrial bargaining, increasingly replaced by bargaining at company level. This is partly because companies have seen the benefits of ensuring that agreements they make with their staff fit the company's position, not that of the lowest common denominator for the industry as a whole. At the same time, companies have begun to develop much more professional industrial relations departments of their own. There is a feeling in these departments that employers' associations often take as their reference the interests of the greater number of less professional small companies.

Employers' associations are still important on the British industrial relations scene; but less important than formerly.

The Confederation of British Industry

Employers have a national organization representing them all; the Confederation of British Industry (CBI).

The CBI represents over 10,000 members directly and speaks for all employing organizations. It has in membership individual companies in manufacturing and in commerce, covers the nationalized industries and includes employers' associations and commercial associations.

The CBI provides valuable services, particularly to its smaller member organizations, but it has no real power over any of its members. Its main function as a conglomerate and uneasy coalition is to represent employing organizations to the rest of the nation in general and to government in particular.

Managers as employees

Most managers are also employees, paid a salary by their organization and needing that salary to maintain their accustomed lifestyle. They are in most cases managers of some employees and themselves managed by someone else. Managers are therefore nearly always involved in industrial relations in at least two ways. They have a major impact on the working conditions of their own employees, and at the same time their working conditions are influenced by their own boss.

A much lower proportion of managers than non-managerial employees belong to trade unions. Yet there are many thousands of managers, some of them highly paid, who are trade union members. There are indeed both separate unions for managers and separate sections of non-managerial unions which managers can join. Managers join trade unions, like any other employees, to obtain their support in discussions with their bosses about industrial relations issues.

In practice, this rarely causes problems. This is a surprise to many Americans, for example, who believe that you are either part of the union or part of management. In Britain many people are happy to be both.

There are occasional conflicts of interest, but these are usually resolved amicably. In some companies, union members who are managers do not attend union meetings when the members are discussing the wage claim they will put to the company; but they attend all the others. They find it possible to act as good union members and yet not breach any confidence they obtain during work.

The real problems arise during an industrial dispute when individuals' loyalties as union members and as members of the management team may be in direct opposition. These can be very tense situations for the individual. Fortunately they are rare.

Management; in summary

We have seen then that management plays a central part in industrial relations but that all managers are not the same. Differences in department and level are important. The way these differences are resolved by senior management creates the 'management style' of the organization as it appears to employees. This has a major influence on whether industrial relations in the organization is good or bad.

Some managements use employers' associations to negotiate and advise on key elements of their employees' terms and conditions of employment. We also noted that managers are also employees, and often union members.

Overall, however, management and the way they treat their subordinates are the vital factors in industrial relations. We will examine the other parties, the legal background and the workplace reality of industrial relations in the following chapters. Finally, we will return to the subject of management to consider how, in light of this information, management develops policies to ensure positive industrial relations within the organization.

3 The Trade Unions

What are trade unions?

There are many definitions of trade unions. These range from the very legalistic to the more practical. The legal definition of a trade union, in the Trade Union and Labour Relations Act 1974, states that a trade union is an organization which 'consists wholly or mainly of workers of one or more descriptions and is an organization whose principal purposes include the regulation of relations between workers of that description or those descriptions and employers or employers' associations'.

As in many other areas, the law is here attempting to draw a clear line where there are many practical variations. It is saying that organizations either are or are not trade unions, whereas in practice organizations may be 'more or less' trade unions.

In practice, there are many elements which constitute 'trade union-ness':

- that there is an organization – not just a group of individuals
- that the organization exists to represent its members to employers (primarily) and to others such as the state, the press and the public
- that the organization's primary interest is in the terms and conditions of employment of its members, which it negotiates or wishes to negotiate with its members' employers
- that the organization is not controlled by those employers
- that the organization is prepared to arrange and

coordinate the breaking of contracts of employment
by its members (in strikes or other industrial action)
where necessary
■ that the organization is a member of the Trades Union
Congress
■ that the organization supports the Labour Party.

Many of the organizations we read about in newspapers
contain all seven elements. Some will have less. Some
organizations that we do not normally think of as trade
unions contain many of these elements.

So the definition of a trade union is complex. It includes,
at the very least, the idea of bargaining collectively on
behalf of its members with their employers. Beyond that
organizations may be more or less totally trade unions –
and that has very little to do with their title, which may
often use other words such as 'association', rather than
'union'.

We are principally concerned here with trade unions that
contain the first five elements. Most of these are also
members of the TUC (the sixth element) and about half of
that group are affiliated to the Labour Party (the seventh).

Trade union members

Just under half the total working population belongs to a
trade union. It is not surprising therefore that 'trade union
members' covers a wide range of people. By the mid 1980s,
nearly a third of all trade union members were women:
nearly 40 per cent of all trade union members were white-
collar workers; the bulk of trade union members worked in
the public sector. Furthermore these groups – women,
white-collar workers and public-sector employees – represent an ever-increasing proportion of the union membership. The traditional stereotype of a male manual worker in
the private engineering industry is outdated.

How many trade union members are there in Britain? It

depends on our first, definitional, point: which organizations you have included. It also depends on when you ask the question. The figure changes continually as new members join and some who are in the unions cease to be members. The official statistics presented by the government's Department of Employment and its predecessors give us the picture shown in Figure 1.

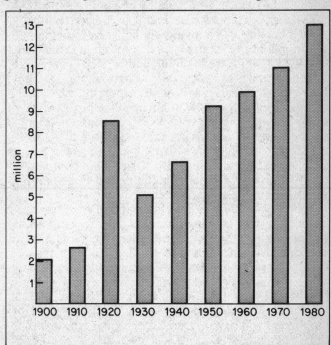

Figure 1 United Kingdom trade union membership at the end of each decade

Figure 1 excludes some 'unions' which are not covered by Department of Employment statistics. Organizations which negotiate collective terms and conditions for doctors, lawyers, policemen and others are excluded. Further, we noted in Chapter 1 that some 12 per cent of the working population are not in employment because they are, for instance, self-employed. Some people, employed in the armed forces or in security, are legally unable to join trade unions. Even though unions have lost members dramatically in the depression of the 1980s, it is still the case that the majority of employees are trade union members. Britain is a highly unionized country.

Membership varies markedly between industries. In traditional heavy industries, such as mining, the docks and the railways, trade union membership is very high; in others, such as shop-work or agriculture, it is low. Fifty years ago there was no air transport industry and no computer industry – now union membership is very high in air transport, but very low in computers. Amongst teachers and nurses it has increased within living memory from low to high. Membership changes over time as well as with industry. It also varies from company to company within the same industry and from group to group within the same company.

People join trade unions for various reasons, some immediate and others more general. The immediate reasons include the wish to influence a pay claim, a threat of redundancy, or some high-handed action by management. It is possible, of course, to respond to these situations by leaving employment. For most people, however, this is not a realistic option. They need a job and other jobs may not be easy to find. Further, most employees will have invested their time in the organization they work for. Leaving will mean they lose seniority, their pension rights may suffer and they will lose certain legal rights. If leaving is not a realistic possibility, collective action through a trade union certainly is. There is much evidence that people join trade unions in increasing numbers when the economy is booming (to make sure they get their share) and in the initial stages of economic decline (for protection). (See Figure 1.)

Union membership is perhaps chiefly determined by the attitude of government and the attitude of managements. If both are supportive, union membership will grow – as it did in the late 1970s. If both are antagonistic, it will decline – as it has in the early 1980s.

Joining a trade union is easy. There are far fewer hurdles to overcome than there are in joining a golf club, for example. It is not true, as some cynical commentators suggest, that a union will take anyone who is 'warm and willing' (i.e. alive and wants to join), but unions will generally want their membership to be as large as possible within the areas they cover – and some unions claim to cover all areas. In most circumstances, a potential member will find that there is a union which is recognized by fellow workers, management and other unions as being appropriate to that particular job.

If the rules governing which union you join and restrictions on who can join are less severe than those of a golf club, we should also add that it's a lot cheaper! A few unions fix their subscriptions at a percentage of their members' salaries – the pilots' union, BALPA, does so and, pilots being as well paid as they are, that makes BALPA a wealthy union. Most unions, however, have subscriptions fixed at certain weekly or monthly sums, adjusted when the union's policy-makers agree to do so. These subscriptions are often no more than the price of a pint of beer. They are significantly lower in Britain than in the rest of Europe. This in turn means that the resources available to the unions are meagre: the services, particularly the professional services, that they can provide are limited; and the unions rely heavily on their lay officials, the unpaid representatives amongst the membership who act as shop stewards or branch officials as well as working at their paid job.

Multi-unionism

Some managers and several industrial relations experts are concerned about the extent of multi-unionism in Britain. By that they mean the situation where several trade unions operate in one employing organization; this is usual in manufacturing or local government, for example. It is unusual in this country for just one union to represent all of one organization's employees. Some experts point to the comparative strike records we looked at in Chapter 1 – compare the position in Japan, where each company has its own union, or West Germany, where each of sixteen industries has its own union – and argue that multi-unionism is a cause. But, as we saw in Chapter 1, there is no simple cause. There is less multi-unionism in the United States and their strike record is much worse than Britain's.

We will look at multi-unionism again from the management viewpoint. From the point of view of the potential member, however, it is hardly important. In most cases any one group of workers is represented by only one union; it is clear which union the employee should join.

Some people join unions for the services they provide. Trade unions give legal support where necessary; they support members who want to take further education or some professional qualifications; they advise on safety matters; many unions even offer discounts on shopping or holidays!

Most members, however, judge their union on what it achieves in negotiations at the workplace. It is the union's ability to defend its members from arbitrary management decisions, and to advance and improve the terms and conditions on which they are employed, that causes most people to join.

Of course some join the union because they believe in the labour movement or because they want to influence decisions made by the TUC. These individuals, who often form the backbone of the union's formal organization, are rare, however. But because most individuals judge their union on its achievements at the workplace, the few who are committed to these wider ideals have a disproportionate influence at higher levels. Union members have been characterized as apathetic – not caring what the union does or says in their name. The truth is that the members are very concerned in their own workplace. Beyond that most members are indifferent to statements made by the distant figures speaking for their union.

Most members, when they talk about their union, are actually thinking of their own local lay representatives. These representatives are fellow workers, employed by the organization they work for as are all the other union members, but chosen to represent particular groups of them to management.

It is difficult to generalize about employee representatives, or *shop stewards* as they are often known. Their function and type are as varied as the members they represent. Even their titles are varied: shop stewards, staff representatives, staff side committee members, corresponding members.

The work of union representatives

While the tasks of employee representatives are extremely varied, nearly all representatives are involved in certain activities:

- making sure everyone who could be in the union is approached to join it
- maintaining interest and enthusiasm by keeping people informed about the work of the union
- alerting members to management action and plans
- representing members' grievances and aspirations to management.

The representatives or shop stewards will carry out these tasks differently. One may simply place notices on a noticeboard and speak to management only when a member has been disciplined; another may call regular meetings of the membership, meet frequently with management and negotiate wages and salaries. There is also a range of other tasks which representatives may perform, including liaison with union officers, distribution of literature, attendance at safety or pension committee meetings; but few representatives will carry out the full range. That would be a full-time job.

There are about 250,000 union representatives in Britain. Most spend on average an hour or so a day of working time on union business, for which they are paid as an employee, and perhaps as much again of their own time, for which they are not paid. Some of them, a few thousand, *are* in fact full-time. It is quite common in a factory or office to have a senior representative who is still paid 'wages' but who in fact works only as a representative. (These senior representatives are often called 'convenors').

The union rules place few restrictions on a representative. This is clear from 'Functions of Shops Stewards' (issued by a union) and the 'Shop Steward's Credentials' (issued by a company) on pp.45–6. These would be typical for a shop steward in manufacturing. Hence the job is often what the individual makes of it.

In summary, the only formal constraints on the employee representatives are:

- they should comply with union rules and policies
- they may not initiate or continue industrial action on behalf of the union
- they must abide by relevant agreements and try to ensure that their members do so too
- they will, when not acting as a shop steward, conform to the same rules as their workmates.

Transport and General Workers' Union
Functions of Shop Stewards: rules and policies

For the purpose of representing membership on matters affecting their employment, a shop steward or equivalent representative shall be elected by the membership in a defined working area or at a branch meeting by a show of hands or ballot as may from time to time be determined.

Special elections shall be held on the requisition of the membership concerned or at defined periods, but in any case elections shall take place at least once every two years. The representative so elected shall be in compliance and act in accordance with union rules and policies.

The regional committee or its authorized subcommittee may have authority to withdraw credentials of a shop steward or equivalent representative in circumstances where it is considered that the representative is not acting in accordance with union rules and policies, subject to the right of appeal as provided for in these rules.

Shop stewards shall receive the fullest support and protection from the union, and immediate inquiry shall be undertaken by the appropriate trade group or district committee into every case of dismissal of a shop steward with a view to preventing victimization, either open or concealed.

Shop stewards are not authorized to initiate or continue industrial action on behalf of the union. This authority is vested only in the general executive committee, its finance and general purposes committee and the general secretary.

Extract from TGWU shop steward's credential card, with acknowledgements.

Example of a shop steward's credentials

The company and trade union jointly agree on the following credentials for Mr/Mrs .... who has been elected to represent the union members in the .... representational area on............ (date).

1 When acting in his/her union capacity he/she shall be subject to the rules and regulations of the union.
2 He/she accepts the duties laid down with the domestic and national procedure agreements in respect of the employees in the above representational area.
3 He/she agrees to abide, and to use his/her best endeavours to see that the members abide, by all agreements (of which he/she will receive copies) between the company and the union, whether present or future, in particular the negotiating procedure for settling issues, hearing objection against disciplinary actions and dismissals.
4 He/she is assured that his/her average earnings will be maintained for the time he/she spends in carrying out his/her duties as defined by the agreements and his/her credentials.
5 Action taken by him/her in good faith in pursuance of his/her duties shall in no way affect his/her employment with the company.
6 In all other respects he/she shall conform to the same working conditions as other employees.

These are not onerous restrictions, particularly considering that even these are sometimes not observed. Most strikes, for example, are impromptu events – over before the formal union structure hears about them.

Employee representatives rarely receive much formal advice on how to do their jobs. Only a minority receive training for the task, although many are given a handbook. Most develop their activities through a combination of learning-by-watching (either the shop stewards they replaced or a senior shop steward or convenor) and from their own assessment of what needs to be done. Little wonder that the job differs so noticeably from one representative to another.

As well as serving his or her workmates, the shop steward is also a representative of the union and an employee. These obligations can pull in different directions.

The workplace representatives discuss, argue and negotiate on behalf of their colleagues with their own management and with more senior managers within the organization. Representatives also meet with representatives from other workgroups. They may be from a different part of the same office or factory or they may be from other workplaces of the same employer. The majority of representatives are members of local committees: staff side committees, office representative committees, joint shop stewards' committees. These will often include representatives from other unions as well as other work areas. Some will be members of wider arrangements: 'combine committees', which include representatives of all the unions and all the workplaces covered by one employer. In many unions the workplace representatives attend regular 'industrial conferences' of their union to consider the union's policy in relation to the particular industries they come from.

These meetings, with other workgroups' representatives, with other people in the union hierarchy and with managers mean that the representative has more information than his fellow workers and often a somewhat different perspective. The representative can develop a position as leader, influencer and persuader.

This is where the representative's position becomes controversial. Some newspapers seem to believe that employee representatives are leading their colleagues astray – particularly when the representatives are called shop stewards!

A more objective view comes from the Royal Commission on Industrial Relations which reported in 1968. Its conclusions are backed up by more recent research:

'Shop stewards are rarely agitators pushing workers towards unconstitutional action. In some instances, they may be the mere mouthpiece of their workgroups. But, quite commonly, they are supporters of order exercising a restraining influence on their members.'

The Commission's Report adds:

'For the most part the shop steward is viewed by others, and views himself, as an accepted and even moderating influence; more of a lubricant than an irritant.'*

Union Structure

So far we have said little about formal union structure. This is because, for the members, the union is usually seen as the representative, and most representatives are integrated only very loosely into the formal structure of the union. Many union rulebooks still pay only scant attention to the workplace representatives, those crucial components of the union's structure.

Those representatives that do get more involved in the union outside the workplace often do so in other positions, as branch secretaries or committee members. It is to these more formal structures that we turn now.

The branches

By now it should be clear that we can rarely generalize about members and shop stewards without risking some large inaccuracies. As the members and repre-

*Report of the Royal Commission on Trade Unions and Employers' Associations (chairman: Lord Donovan), 1968.

sentatives form the bedrock of the union it follows that we will not be able to generalize about the official union structures any more easily.

There are several broad similarities, particularly among the unions that contain the first six of our elements of trade union-ness. In the first place they operate through some form of branch structure. Branches are the immediate unit to which all members belong. Most are based on a geographical area or workplace, some are occupational (for instance, senior staff branch), others are based on an industry. They all have regular, often monthly, meetings which all members are entitled to attend – but which few actually do.

The low level of attendance is hardly surprising, if our understanding of the members' objectives is correct. They are mainly interested in the union as a negotiating body at the workplace, not as a formal bureaucracy. They put their views through the shop steward or representative, not through the branch.

It is through the branches that the shop stewards or employee representatives are linked to the formal union structure. Many of the representatives also hold some branch office: branch chairman, branch secretary, treasurer. In the public sector, which tends to have workplace-based branches, 'employee representative' and 'branch official' are often different titles for the same job.

What does the branch do? It is often used, particularly in the older unions which recruit mainly manual workers, as a financial unit, where the shop stewards can pay in the subscriptions collected at their place of work. Generally speaking, however, 'subs' are increasingly being deducted from the employee's pay by the company, which then passes the total sum on to the union offices. This is known as the 'check-off' system.

One of the key functions of the branch is exchange of information. In workplace-based branches this will be information about the activities of the employer, or perhaps about different groups of managers in a large public sector undertaking. In geographically based branches this will be comparative information, so that members can assess how their terms and conditions compare with those in other companies.

The branch can play an important role in coordinating the activities of the members. It is often the branch that plans approaches to management on various topics, gathers material for wage and salary claims and organizes action in the event of a dispute.

The branch is also the fundamental building block in the structure of the union. At the branch, members will discuss and debate any issue that they themselves decide to be important; here also the resolutions which eventually form the policy of the whole union will be formulated. Each union has its own arrangements about how these issues are progressed up from the branch level but all unions are committed to the concept that they are democratic organizations, controlled and directed by the membership. The control and direction are based on the branches.

Regional Structure

The actions of the branches are progressed through, or reviewed by, the next level of the union hierarchy. For most of at least the larger unions, the regional (or divisional or district) level is an important intermediary between the branches and the headquarters. It is at this level that most unions place their junior level full-time officials. These regional posts can command a good deal of power and often be substantially independent of the directions of the headquarters officials.

Other unions, in the civil service, for example, do not have any regional structure. In these cases, branches are grouped into sections covering similar types of branch throughout the country. Other unions again, such as the Transport and General Workers, have both regional and sectional groupings.

Trade union headquarters

The headquarters of the union will in most cases house a general secretary, responsible for the administration of the union, some national officers and a number of service departments. These might include some or all of the following: membership and organization department, research department, a computer section, a finance department, training and education departments, public relations, information and publications departments, health and safety sections, insurance and superannuation departments and a secretariat.

Depending on the size and complexity of the union, and upon its history and constitutional arrangements, headquarters can loom very large in union affairs.

General Secretary

Whereas for most members their union is the shop steward, for the media the union is the general secretary. These are the names and faces that we see in our newspapers every morning and on our television screens every night. Their real power varies.

In a union like the National Union of Seamen, with members spread around the globe, often away from the United Kingdom for long periods of time, there is little alternative to a powerful general secretary running the union and negotiating most major deals. Another union which has superficial similarities, the British Airline Pilots' Association, in fact has many highly educated, articulate and literate members with plenty of time available to get involved in many of the union's activities. Here the general secretary has less opportunity to dictate matters.

General secretaries are often elected by the full membership of the union. In many unions, once elected, they are in post for life. Some unions require their general secretaries to stand in regular elections every few years. And in others the general secretary is appointed, not elected.

Other Officials

Below the general secretary there will be other officials. A few unions, like the Amalgamated Engineering Union (AEU) and the Electrical Electronic Telecommunications and Plumbing Union (EETPU), have full-time executive councils elected directly by the membership. Most unions have several national officials working from headquarters.

Full-time officials are not, in most cases, elected. But in some unions, particularly the more traditional craft unions, all the full-time officials are elected and subject to periodic re-election. In other unions only the very top posts, such as general secretary, are elected – and that election often lasts for life. In some unions all the officials are appointed without election; in others some are elected and some appointed.

Elections traditionally took place at branch meetings. As we have seen, these are often attended only by a small number of active members. Although others could attend, the system has nonetheless been criticized as being undemocratic. Under government legislative pressure many unions have moved to postal ballots sent to and from the members' homes. The government has made money available to the unions who wish to use this more expensive approach.

There are over 400 unions in Great Britain. They employ over 3,000 full-time officials. Most of these officials are drawn from the membership they represent, although, especially among the white-collar unions and in the civil service, there are an increasing number of well-educated 'professional' officials being appointed. These officials, with one or two exceptions, are not highly paid. They do important and demanding jobs that keep them involved well into the evenings, attending branch or committee meetings or recruiting and negotiating. They often work weekends, on union training courses or at conferences, and most of them do much travelling around the country. The vast majority are dedicated people working hard to support and improve the lot of their members.

There are over ten million union members in the United Kingdom. Other countries, including West Germany and the United States, have fewer members but more full-time officials.

The union rely heavily on 250,000 lay officials (branch officers and workplace representatives), and now about half as many workplace safety representatives too. These people are the backbone of the trade union movement.

Policy-making

Whether appointed or elected, the job of full-time officials is to carry out union policy. They do not make that policy. In all unions the supreme policy-making body consists of a group of elected lay members. Sometimes they will meet at national conferences; once a year or once every two years. These may be gatherings of some hundreds of members representing everyone in the union. Sometimes they will be national committees; smaller groups but again of lay members. Most unions have a system whereby resolutions can be originated in the branches and passed up through the regional or sectional structures to industrial interest-group conferences or to the full policy-making conference. The extent to which these policy-making bodies do in practice restrict the action of full-time officials varies.

'Feds' and 'confeds'

Unions often act independently, but they can also operate jointly. There are arrangements within many organizations for unions to work together, going under a variety of names, such as joint shop stewards committees or the trade union side of a particular local council. There are joint groupings at national or industrial level in which, for example, all the Post Office unions or all the shipbuilding and engineering unions meet and liaise regularly. Such bodies are known as 'federations' or 'confederations'.

The Trades Union Congress

Between 80 and 90 of the 400 trade unions registered with the certification officer are affiliated to the main national grouping of unions: the Trades Union Congress, or TUC as it is more commonly known. These unions include well over 90 per cent of all members.

We are so used to mention of the TUC in our newspapers and on television that we are often unaware of how unusual it is. Only a minority of countries have a single organization to represent and speak so authoritatively for all their trade unions. Other countries have national federations which represent much smaller percentages of the workforce, or are split along religious, political or occupational lines. The British TUC covers all major and most medium-sized unions in the country and also includes a good representation of the small ones. It is a single body speaking for most trade unionists.

The Trades Union Congress does play some part in the occasional membership disputes between unions. In these rare, but often bitter, disputes as to who should recruit certain members, the TUC now has a well-established procedure for settlement. The TUC also provides much information to its constituent unions. And it provides an extensive shop steward and safety representative training programme through a range of further education facilities.

These are valuable but peripheral services. The main function of the TUC lies not in its concern with the affairs of its own constituents but in its position as spokesman and representative for the union movement: in its outward rather than its inward task. The TUC has little real power over its member unions but a great deal of influence as the voice of the labour movement. Few major governmental decisions are taken without some consultation within the Trades Union Congress, though governments differ in how much they allow the TUC view to influence them. The TUC is represented on many important committees and public bodies. It has a major input into the financing, organization and policies of the Labour Party (see Chapter 4).

It is a mistake to see the TUC as an overall umbrella organization controlling its members. Rather it is a mouthpiece for the policies and influence that its members wish to pursue.

TUC structure

What is the structure that the TUC has developed to ensure that it represents its members unions' views accurately? Not surprisingly, the TUC's internal arrangements mirror many aspects of individual union structures. Instead of individual members, the TUC has unions: paying and sending delegates to the annual congress on the basis of size.

The congress meets alternately in Blackpool or Brighton, in September of each year, to establish policy. The votes of each union are weighted according to its size. This is known as the 'block vote': each union voting as if all its members were in agreement on the

issue under debate. Organizationally the TUC is led by
the general council – the fifty-two senior union officials
who meet monthly at the TUC headquarters in London
to conduct business between the annual congresses.
This is in practice mostly undertaken by a number of
subcommittees and the specialist staff that service them.
The specialist full-time staff are, as are most unions,
headed by a general secretary. The TUC does have a
regional structure but it is very weak. It also has some
400 trades councils operating as its local agents. Their
success depends on the enthusiasm of the local union
officials, lay and full-time, and some are extremely
active. The links to the national body are often weak,
however.

In many respects the functions and powers of the
Trades Union Congress are similar to those of the CBI
outlined in Chapter 2:

- the main function is to represent the views of member organizations
- the main target for influence is government
- special services are provided for members, particularly for smaller member organizations
- very little power is exercised over members, except
  by persuasion.

4   The State in Industrial Relations

This chapter examines the role of the third major party in industrial relations. The word 'state' rather than the more familiar word 'government' is used for two main reasons. The first is that 'state' is more neutral: it does not refer to any particular party or power group, whereas the word 'government' may well be read as meaning the group that is in office now. The second reason is that it is a wider term: it covers all the various organizations that are directly employed by us, the taxpayers. Thus, it includes the machinery and employees of the government in civil service and related advisory and specialist organizations – there are quite a few of these in the industrial relations sphere.

The state has four functions in industrial relations:

- it is a major employer
- it is manager of the economy
- it creates laws
- it provides specialist services.

We will examine each in turn.

The state as employer

The percentage of the workforce employed directly or indirectly by the state is a matter of definition.

It depends to some extent on how we define such words as 'employed', 'directly' and 'indirectly'. We could argue that between 10 per cent and 20 per cent of all employees are employed directly by the state,

	Percentage of employment
Agriculture, forestry and fishing	1.6
Mining and quarrying	1.5
Manufacturing	30.1
Construction	5.6
Gas, electricity and water	1.5
Transport and communications	6.6
Distribution	12.3
Insurance, banking, etc.	5.6
Professional and Scientific services	16.4
Miscellaneous	10.1
National government	2.7
Local government	4.3
Armed forces	1.4

Table 2 *Employment by sectors*

depending upon whether or not we included local authority workers.

We could argue, too, that a further 10 per cent to 20 per cent are employed indirectly by the state, depending upon which nationalized and semi-nationalized companies we include, and whether we added in organizations such as the motorway construction companies which work almost entirely for the state.

In addition, there are a substantial number of firms in the private, non-state sector which provide goods or services, like uniforms, equipment or machinery, almost entirely to nationalized industries such as the British Coal, the health service, the fire service or the armed forces. Perhaps their employees should be counted in, too. Whichever way you add up the figures, it is clear that the state is the dominant employer in Britain now.

The Whitley Committee

The civil service and many other parts of the state machinery conduct their industrial relations on the Whitley pattern. The Whitley Committee was set up and reported immediately after the First World War. The committee was asked to make recommendations about industrial relations, and its brief 27-page report has probably had more impact on public sector industrial relations than the millions of words that have been written since. Whitley and his committee recommended a system of joint councils at national, district and local levels meeting frequently to discuss industrial relations issues. Employers and unions would each be represented on all levels, and neither would be allowed to outvote the other. Thus, any changes in employment conditions would have to be agreed by both sides or they would not take place. These recommendations were adopted wholeheartedly by the government of the day. For more than half a century, all aspects of employment have been discussed through just such joint machinery in nearly all areas where the state is directly involved.

Requirements to establish Whitley-style machinery were included by successive governments in Acts of Parliament setting up new services or nationalizing certain industries. The Whitley Committee had aimed its recommendations rather more at the private than the public sector, but its ideas were taken up in full in only a minority of cases. Advantages of the Whitley system include:

- the recognition of the legitimacy of trade union interest in a wide range of subjects, combined with a formal channel for that interest to be expressed
- the flexibility of the system
- regular meetings at all levels to improve communication and reduce the possibility of conflict over important issues

- stable and continuing procedures to reduce the need or demand for non-constitutional ways of raising issues (strikes or go-slows, for example).

Despite these advantages, the state has had its problems in industrial relations over recent years. The last decade has seen industrial disputes not only in the traditionally difficult nationalized industries, such as mining, steel and the railways, but in many other areas. Groups of workers previously thought to be antagonistic to trade unions became involved in industrial action: civil servants, firemen, local authority workers, teachers.

There are various reasons for this increased tendency to use industrial action in the public sector. These include:

- increasing pressure by government on public sector costs (see p.63 later in this chapter)
- increasing numbers of younger workers employed in the public sector, bringing in different objectives, educational backgrounds and philosophies
- declining status of many of these sectors – employees in them are now seen as just another part of the workforce rather than as a sub-elite
- the impact of growing prosperity in the private sector which has led to a relative decline in the financial position of many public sector workers
- the impact of pay policies (see p.63 later in this chapter) which have been most restrictive in those areas most under government control.

These partial explanations leave us a long way short of understanding why there is industrial action. They do help us to understand, however, why the public sector is becoming more like the private sector in its industrial relations. It sometimes looks much worse, of course. Because there is only one employer, because there are large numbers of employees involved and because action in the public sector usually has a very direct effect upon the public, strikes attract much press attention.

In many ways the state, as employer, has peculiar difficulties to face. The state is not able to act as other employers do. There is a political dimension. The low wages paid in many branches of the civil service, in the health service and by local authorities seem to be acceptable to the general public.

It would not be seen as acceptable, however, for public sector employees to be 'sacked' arbitrarily. In employment terms alone, the state has led the field in such areas as trade union recognition, employment guarantees and pension provisions. There have recently been moves to reduce this role and for the state to adopt employment criteria similar to those in the private sector.

With so much employment directly or indirectly controlled by the state, its wages and salaries and indeed all aspects of its industrial relations are an important part of its economic management function.

The state as economic manager

One of the prime duties of the state is to manage the economy. This has an indirect effect on industrial relations, as well as some very direct implications.

We will look at these implications; at how the state has affected industrial relations in its attempts to manage the economy (particularly through incomes policies), and at the relationship between industrial relations and politics and the objectives that the state may be trying to achieve.

The interrelationship of the national economy and industrial relations is an extensive and complex area. Any comprehensive summary would be longer than this book. To give a few examples:

- government action which affects employment will

affect the bargaining power of the unions, or might make the parties concentrate on different issues, such as redundancy agreements
- changes to national insurance might encourage or discourage individuals who want to become self-employed
- government support of subsidies for particular industries or companies will change employment prospects both there and in supplier organizations
- changing inflation rates will have a key influence on employees' expectations in the annual pay negotiations.

There are many others.

We should also remember that, because the state owns or controls much of the British economy, it has a very immediate influence over it.

Of course, the extent of the state's ownership is a matter of political debate. There is a fundamental difference in the Conservative Party's approach to this topic, which emphasizes the need for market competition and decentralization, and that of the Labour Party, which emphasizes planning and coordination. Whichever party is in power, however, the United Kingdom is likely to be running a 'mixed economy' with a substantial proportion of the economy under direct government ownership and another substantial section privately owned.

The government also has more than a little influence in those sectors which it does not own. Many businessmen believe that the government's influence is crucial; it determines the rates at which money can be borrowed, the opportunities to expand, the industries that will be viable in the future.

All these factors will affect industrial relations within organizations, though they will affect them somewhat indirectly. The state's management of the economy does, however, also relate very directly to industrial relations. Even before the Second World War, the state was liable to become involved in industrial relations as part of its attempts to manage the economy. Since 1945, such involvement has been seen as vital: most politicians would echo Conservative Prime Minister Edward Heath, who said: 'I consider industrial relations to be absolutely crucial to economic progress.'

In particular most governments, and not just those in Britain, have seen the control of the financial outcome of collective bargaining as central to the economy. By the outcome I mean, of course, the wages and salaries that employers and employees negotiate. In practice, this has meant that governments have attempted to influence the result of those negotiations.

They have used a variety of methods. These include:

- exhortation and persuasion
- statutory laws backed by legal sanctions on those who exceed the laid-down limits
- negotiating themselves with the central employees' and employers' bodies (the TUC and the CBI) and leaving it to them, and to public opinion, to control the negotiators.
- using their control over the public sector to limit pay increases there, with the expectation that increases in the private sector will follow suit.

It is usual for a combination of these methods to be involved.

Incomes policies

These attempts to restrict the financial outcome of collective negotiations are given the generic title of 'incomes policies'. They are the subject of a fierce and continuing political and economic debate. Argument centres on a few key questions:

- Do incomes policies work? Or are wage and salary levels a response to economic conditions rather than a prime cause of them?
- Are incomes policies fair? Why should earned income be restricted when unearned income from shareholding, etc. is not? Isn't it easier for the highly-paid to protect their increases by taking them in kind (such as a bigger car rather than more cash) whereas the low-paid have no option?
- Are incomes policies effective? Do they in fact achieve their objectives?

Incomes policies are a subject of much debate and are seen differently by different negotiators. On both the trade union and the company sides, there are those who see incomes policies as the opposite of negotiation: 'If a 3 per cent limit is set, we just get together and rubber stamp the 3 per cent for a particular organization.' Others see it as a challenge: 'If we're restricted to 3 per cent on the pay package, what else can we do?' This group would start looking at non-pay benefits such as cheap travel to work or at new areas of negotiation like increasing training opportunities.

Precise incomes policies, enforced by law if necessary, work well only in certain circumstances. These are:

- where the state exercises a great deal of control over many aspects of working life, as it does in the Communist countries of Eastern Europe or some of the capitalist countries of the Far East (e.g. Singapore)
- or where countries have small working populations and a high degree of 'social consensus' (such as Holland or the Scandinavian nations) or agreement about society's objectives.

Incomes policies work less well in large, complex societies where there is a much lower degree of social consensus. Britain is just such a country.

What is common to most countries in which incomes policies can be seen to be effective is that they have a centralized bargaining structure (i.e. pay and conditions are set for everyone by just a few overall meetings). Here, we need only note that in Britain and other countries with decentralized bargaining (i.e. a large number of negotiations over pay and conditions), incomes policies have to grapple with many conflicting criteria:

- how to reconcile simplicity and the ability to control with flexibility (if everyone gets just 3 per cent that's easy to check; if all sorts of groups are allowed more or less, it becomes more difficult)
- how to reconcile strictness with fairness (if everyone is allowed 3 per cent this year, should workers who gained no increase last year be allowed more?)
- how to reconcile help for the low paid with the need to maintain differentials (3 per cent of £5 is only £0.15; 3 per cent of £1,000 is £30 – so the worse off get relatively even poorer)
- how to reconcile timings with justice (if your factory and mine both agree to a 10 per cent increase, and yours came into effect last week and mine next, I will not be too happy with a 3 per cent limit imposed this week).

There are other problems. In particular, an increasing proportion of the income of many white-collar workers and managers is being taken in non-wage items such as private medical insurance, motor cars, season-ticket allowances, luncheon vouchers, bonuses. These are difficult items for anyone wanting to monitor labour cost increases to control.

The political connection

Despite the above problems, many argue that some sort of incomes policy is either inevitable or desirable. It is a debate with many political overtones, so this is a good point at which to raise the issue of the relationship between industrial relations and politics.

We emphasized, right at the beginning of our analysis of industrial relations, that the subject is value-laden. How you react to events, and the overall view that you will take of the subject, is strongly influenced by your values. The same is true for politics.

The same values which lead an individual to support one political party or another will often lead that individual to take a view of industrial relations that coincides with the views of the chosen party. There is an affinity of views between the Labour Party and the trade unions and between the Conservative Party and the employers.

We have already noted (p.54) that Britain is unusual in Europe in having trade unions and political parties which, with the exception of Northern Ireland, are not divided on religious lines. But, whether we like it or not, there are divides.

Many trade unions expressly avoid political affiliation – less than half are linked to a political party. All those which are linked, however, are linked to the Labour Party.

The links between the two are ideological, historical, financial and economic. Ideologically, both are committed to increasing equality, to social ownership and to democratic controls. Historically, the Labour Party was founded by the trade unions to fight, amongst other things, for trade union rights. Financially, the trade unions provide the bulk of the Labour Party's income and a lot of organizational support. And in terms of management of the economy, the trade unions and the Labour Party have similar objectives.

Both owners and managers of business and the Conservative Party are ideologically committed to the present capitalist economy in which private businesses may thrive, and to the importance of incentives (in terms of financial reward) for those who invest their money. Historically, there are links between them going back several centuries. Financially, businessmen, big and small, are the major supporters of the Conservative Party. And again, this party and owners and managers of business have similar objectives in the management of the economy.

The position of the other parties, such as the Liberal Party and the Social Democratic Party, is less clear or perhaps, they might say, more independent. Nevertheless, their view of the way the state should manage the economy will be crucial to the way they are viewed by businessmen and trade unions.

Let us move down from our abstraction, the 'state', to the various party governments which have been in power. Each will, amongst other things, be attempting to meet general economic objectives.

Four economic objectives are often seen as crucial:

- full employment. Times are changing, and full employment (which means in practice a very low rate of unemployment) is no longer attainable. Perhaps 'lower unemployment' is a more realistic objective
- a positive balance of payments: what the country is buying in from abroad should not cost more than what the country sells abroad
- control of inflation: keeping price rises down to an acceptable level
- economic growth: so that the country as a whole becomes richer.

The relative importance attached to these four objectives will vary at different times. Any one party may, when in government, concentrate on one objective at the expense of others. Thus, some would argue that Harold Wilson's Labour government in 1969 concentrated on the country's balance of payments at the expense of controlling inflation. Some would argue that Margaret Thatcher's Conservative government from 1979 has concentrated on controlling inflation at the expense of full employment. What a government concentrates on will be determined by the general economic situation and by its own view of that situation.

Industrial relations is a crucial area in which management of the economy can meet success or failure. The link between industrial relations and politics influences political parties' views of economic objectives. To take one example, the Labour Party, with its strong trade union ties, would be more inclined to take action to alleviate unemployment (however much that may be a short-term palliative) than would the Conservative Party.

So industrial relations affects the state's economic objectives and influences its success.

The state as law-giver

One of the key functions of the state is to enact laws regulating the conduct of the people and organizations it controls. Britain, unlike the majority of countries, does not have a written constitution. Our laws have evolved through a combination of judicial decision-making and statute.

Many aspects of industrial relations, including our industrial system and the trade unions, existed before the state had passed any laws relating to them. Laws passed in the nineteenth century, before the mass of people were directly represented in Parliament, tended to restrict union activities. The unions were forced to campaign against such legislation and, in 1902, established their own party, the Labour Party, to help them do it.

Voluntarism

Over the years the trade unions developed the approach known as 'voluntarism'. 'Free collective bargaining' in negotiating is the best-known feature of the voluntarist system, by which unions and employers are free to fix wages and working conditions between them. Voluntarism implies:

- the independence of industrial relations from government control
- self-reliance of the trade unions – free to conduct their affairs as they see fit
- a distrust of legislation.

The voluntary system is strongly rooted in the traditions of the trade union movement, but it is not an approach adopted solely by the unions. As an 'ideology' it has found easy acceptance with managers. Governments, too, have tended to accept the 'hands off' role that this ideology prescribes for them. When they have not, as during the period of the 1971 Industrial Relations Act, there was considerable evidence of connivance between union and managements to preserve the voluntary character of their industrial relations arrangements.

For both managements and unions, voluntarism means that they have more freedom to conduct their affairs, there are few penalties when they break agreements and arrangements can be changed more easily. The main disadvantage is that the two sides have no recourse to anyone else if the agreements are broken; they have to rely on their own power and skill in all cases.

Since the mid 1960s, however, the concept of the abstention of the law from Britain's industrial relations has been a matter of intense debate. Table 3 details some of the legislation passed since 1970.

1959
Terms and Conditions of Employment Act

1963, 1972
Contracts of Employment Acts

1965
Redundancy Payments Act

1970
Equal Pay Act

1971
Industrial Relations Act

1972
Industry Act

1973, 1981
Employment and Training Acts

1974
Health and Safety at Work Act

1974, 1976
Trade Union and Labour Relations Acts

1975
Sex Discrimination Act

1975, 1978
Employment Protection Acts

1976
Race Relations Act

1980
Employment Act

1982
Employment Act

1984
Trade Union Act

Table 3 *Industrial relations legislation since 1970*

It has been argued that there is very little of voluntarism remaining. We have already seen that, through its role as dominant employer and via its management of the economy, the state has a substantial controlling influence on the hard cash outcomes of collective bargaining. We noted in Chapter 3 that certain elements of the way the trade unions operate are controlled by law, and some of the laws in Table 3 have added to that control. We can see from the list of legislation since 1970 that, distrust it as they may, the parties to industrial relations are having to deal with an increasing amount of legislation.

It is still possible to argue that something of voluntarism remains. Those who make this case would point to four specific areas (although they would have to allow exceptions in each case):

- contractual freedom
- freedom of bargaining arrangements
- the non-legal nature of agreements
- freedom to take industrial action.

Contractual freedom remains because most elements of the contract of employment are left to the two sides to agree.

Some legal minimum wages, in a few small industries, are set by bodies known as wages councils. Some people have restrictions on their working hours built-in by the law – lorry drivers and pilots, for example. There are a few legal requirements in all contracts of employment, on matters like notice periods on termination of the contract. In general, however, it is still the case in Britain, in contrast to many other countries, that there are very few legal restrictions on the terms of the contract of employment. Employers and employees may agree on any rate of pay, any hours of work and any amount of holidays that they wish.

Freedom of bargaining arrangements also remains. The law has restricted the way agreements are made in a very few particulars. Again, the wages council industries are an exception. Otherwise, managements can bargain with any union, any number of unions, or with none. There can be recourse to independent arbitrators when negotiations are stuck – or not. Bargains can be made at national, regional or local level, or in each individual department. Management and unions are free to choose.

The non-legal nature of agreements is assumed. The negotiators can choose to make their agreements legally binding but very few, if any, do so. Indeed, between 1971 and 1974, when the law was changed so that the assumption was that most agreements were legally binding unless otherwise stated, the vast majority of agreements included a clause stating specifically that they were binding in honour only.

Freedom of industrial action also remains. The legislation has reduced the type of industrial action that the union side can take without fear of penalty but has left most industrial action still exempt from claims for damages. The union cannot, in most cases, be sued for damages that the strike or go-slow or overtime ban has caused. And where the unions can be sued – where for example the action is not specifically directed against the strikers' own employer – the state has left it to the employer or a third party to take action. The state itself will not get involved.

The state as provider of specialist services

The state provides many specialist services in the industrial relations area. These range from broad-range surveys and reports to detailed intervention in difficult situations.

A key part of the state's function is to manage the economy. If good industrial relations are vital to such management, then it makes sense for the state to do what it can to foster good industrial relations. This is apart from any views about reducing the misery caused by industrial conflict or the rights of people at work.

Direct services provided by the state are the industrial tribunals or 'courts', the Central Arbitration Committee (CAC), the Advisory Conciliation and Arbitration Service (ACAS) and a plethora of regular and occasional commissions, inquiries and committees. All these bodies play a direct part in industrial relations by intervening in situations which have become difficult.

There are also a host of indirect services provided by the Department of Employment, the National Economic Development Council, the Manpower Services Commission and the commissions on equal rights for women and for minority ethnic groups.

What conclusions can we draw from all this? The state is a major employer, indeed by far *the* major employer: in this case, the state is one of the two key parties in industrial relations. The state is required to manage the economy; therefore it is inevitably involved in influencing the atmosphere and often constraining the results of collective bargaining. The state makes the laws; in industrial relations, as in other areas, the state decides upon the legal framework. And the state provides specialist industrial relations services to those involved, to help them in difficult times.

The state sets the framework and is a major influence on industrial relations. It is crucial to our understanding of the subject.

5 The Law and Collective Bargaining

Compared to most countries, the law plays a small part in British industrial relations. Even in Britain, however, it is an important element in the relationship between managements and trade unions and between managers and employees. This chapter looks at the collective relationship: the way law structures industrial relations at the management-union level.

The sources of the law

There are two sources of law. First, common law, or judge-made law; and second, statute law, or laws made by Parliament.

Common law has developed over the centuries. There is no written constitution in Britain, but the courts have traditionally been prepared to insist on standards such as fairness and equity between individuals. Over time, they have built up a body of cases, or 'precedents' as they are called, which lay down principles to be followed by subsequent courts.

Statute law, by contrast, is legislation which has been enacted by Parliament. An enormous amount of legislation goes through Parliament every year. As we saw in Chapter 4, however, it is only recently that statute law has made any significant impact on industrial relations.

Industrial tribunals

Legal regulation of industrial matters is grounded in both common law and statute law. Disputes arising out of statutory provisions which confer rights on individual workers are usually referred to industrial tribunals (ITs). These were established by Parliment in 1965. They comprise a lawyer-chairman and two 'sidesmen'; one from the employee's side and one from the management side. They hear cases as individuals, not representatives, and the vast majority of their verdicts are unanimous. The sidesmen bring a knowledge of industry into the deliberations. The range of subjects covered by the ITs, their 'jurisdiction', now covers the subjects noted in Table 4. With a few exceptions, these are issues which arise between management and employees (or people who want to be or have just ceased to be employees). An individual or a company who is unsatisfied with the decision at an industrial tribunal can appeal to the Employment Appeal Tribunal, which is constituted along similar lines.

Industrial relations problems are considered by specialized tribunals and not ordinary courts because a faster, cheaper, informal and more down-to-earth approach is required. If the dispute is about, say, dismissal of an employee, and the remedy might be his or her re-engagement by the company, it would not be practical to wait many months for a hearing, or to make the hearing so expensive that the employee cannot afford it, or so formal that he cannot put his own case, or so remote from his everyday experience that the issues are not understood.

Codes of practice

Parliament has also recognized the particular problems posed by industrial relations in its use of 'codes of practice'. These are short, practical guidelines, usually issued with authority conferred by an Act of Parliament. The Secretary

Industrial tribunals cover claims in the following areas:

- unfair dismissal
- redundancy payments
- consultation with recognized unions over redundancies and protection of employment
- statement of particulars of employment
- guaranteed pay
- suspension on medical grounds
- maternity rights (pay and return to work)
- trade union membership and activities
- time off for union duties/activities, public duties, and to look for new work when redundant, and ante-natal care
- itemized pay statements
- written reasons for dismissal
- employee rights on insolvency
- equal pay
- sex discrimination
- race discrimination
- appeals against improvement and prohibition notices under the Health and Safety at Work Act
- use of employer's premises for union ballots
- exclusion or expulsion from union
- appeals against industrial levies
- Docks and Harbours Act regulations

Table 4 *Jurisdiction of industrial tribunals*

of State for Employment and the Advisory, Conciliation and Arbitration Service have authority to issue such codes. They are not legally enforceable but can be used as evidence in court. They operate in the same way as the Highway Code. It is not unlawful to ignore the Highway Code, but the police can argue in court that your failure to follow the code is convincing evidence of your having committed an offence (such as dangerous driving).

There is a general code of practice on good industrial relations and other codes on disciplinary practices and procedures, disclosure of information, time-off facilities for shop stewards, picketing and the closed shop.

Voluntarism and the law

We saw in Chapter 4 that Britain has enjoyed a long history of voluntarism in industrial relations.

A government discussion paper in 1981 summarized the traditional position of the law in industrial relations:

> The way in which the law on industrial action has developed so far in this country has been characteristic of our industrial relations as a whole. Compared with most other countries, there has traditionally been a minimum of legal interference and regulation. The conduct of our industrial relations is basically voluntary.

The government was arguing that, of the enormous amount of industrial relations law enacted since the 1960s, most has been aimed at improving protection for individual employees against arbitrary action on the part of managements. The collective relationships between managements and trade unions remain basically unfettered by law.

The status of trade unions

We examined the legal definitions of a trade union on p.37. The key point about those definitions is that a combination of workers is regarded as a legal entity. The law regards the whole group of employees, the union, as a single body capable of making contracts, owning property and so on. These bodies are legally required to keep proper accounts. Additional rights accrue in certain circumstances: first, where the union is registered as independent and second, where the union is recognized by the management of an organization for negotiating and consultation purposes.

Unions can register as independent with the government-appointed certification officer. This officer keeps the rule books and accounts of all unions and can, if requested, issue certificates of independence to unions which satisfy certain criteria. These are that they are firmly established bodies, independent (particularly financially) of the control and influence of employers with whom they deal.

Recognition, on the other hand, comes direct from the management with whom unions wish to negotiate. With recognition come additional legal rights for the union and its members that we will examine shortly. First, however, the point has to be made that recognition of a trade union can be inferred from management action, as well as arising from a specific union agreement. Of course, if management signs a recognition agreement the issue is clear-cut. However, should managers in an organization refer continually to shop stewards to help them resolve problems, legally they will be deemed to have recognized the union even though no agreement has been signed.

The rights which unions can claim vary depending upon whether or not they are registered as independent and whether or not they are recognized. We will look at:

- the rights of members
- the rights of union representatives
- rights to information and consultation.

The rights of members

Rights to join a trade union and take part in trade union activities are protected by law. It is unlawful for a manager to take any discriminatory action against an employee who wants to, or does, join an independent trade union. Nor can management take discriminatory action against an employee who wants to take part in some union activity, such as attending a meeting, if that activity takes place outside working hours, at a tea or lunch break for example, or during working hours with a manager's consent.

It is possible for management to dismiss an employee who refuses to join a union, but only in particular cases where there is a union membership agreement with the union. These, known as 'closed shop' agreements, require everyone in a work area to be a union member. A dismissal for not belonging to the union will be held to be fair only where a very substantial majority of employees have been shown to be in favour of the closed shop, by a secret ballot.

The rights of union representatives

The rights of union representatives are more extensive than those of ordinary members. In addition to the right to take part in union activities, employee representatives at workplaces where the union is recognized can take time off for trade union duties (the management must pay for this time at the normal rate). We saw on p.44 that many representatives spend a large proportion of working hours on union business. Not all union business can be classified as 'duties'; the law restricts that phrase to actions which are concerned directly with industrial relations issues at the workplace. Those union matters which are more general, such as attending union conferences, are excluded. In practice, however, many managements are more generous than they need to be under the strict letter of the law in allowing union representatives time off with pay.

Union representatives also have other rights. They

are, for example, entitled to time off, with pay, for industrial relations training. Time off for such training, if it is approved by the representative's own union or the TUC, cannot lawfully be refused by management. Management may ask to see a syllabus, and can defer the time off if there are too many representatives away at once or if loss of the representatives would have a serious effect on the work. Otherwise, they must allow the time off.

The representatives also have another advantage, though it is a recommendation in a code of practice and not part of the law. This is that they should not be dismissed until management has notified their full-time official. This means that, although they are subject to the same disciplinary rules as all other employees, there is an opportunity for an experienced union official to satisfy him or herself that the representative has not been victimized for undertaking the union job.

Rights to information and consultation

In addition to these, as it were, personal rights, unions have other more general support from the law. They have the right to information to help them negotiate and in certain circumstances the right to be consulted. The right to disclosure of information is, in effect, severely restricted by a number of clauses which exclude, for example:

- information that would be difficult to obtain
- information which might cause injury to the business if disclosed
- information which was obtained in confidence.

The right of the union to be consulted arises in very specific circumstances where the union is independent and recognized. Managers must consult with properly appointed union safety representatives. They must consult with the union prior to declaring redundancies.

To summarize, we can see that while the law accepts trade unions as corporate entities it places very few restrictions upon them. It does, however, give union members and officials some limited rights, designed to support collective bargaining between unions and management.

Strikes

What happens when collective bargaining breaks down and there is a strike? The right to withdraw one's labour – or to strike – is widely regarded in Britain as a right well worth protecting. Parliament has long supported this right and made legislative provision for it.

In most Western countries now, employees are given the right to strike (though, naturally, the exact form of the right varies between nations). The British system, with no written constitution, makes it difficult to establish a specific 'right to strike'. What we have instead is a 'negative right' – unions are, in certain cases, protected from the possibility that they may be sued, and bankrupted, if strikes are called in their name.

This is done by provision of a legal immunity. Union funds are protected (or 'immune') from civil proceedings taken against them in certain strike situations. In such situations, if the union, or more realistically an official acting in the name of the union, induces breaches of contract by calling a strike, the union cannot be sued for any damages caused by those broken contracts (though union officials are still subject to the criminal law).

The immunity depends upon the strike being called 'in contemplation or furtherance of a trade dispute'. This phrase is known as 'the golden formula'. In practice, nearly all strikes have been covered by it. It is

possible to conceive of strikes called for political purposes but these are extremely rare in Britain. Most
union officials would argue that (in their perception at
least) practically every strike is called in contemplation
or furtherance of a trade dispute; but a recent Act of
Parliament has redefined the golden formula to exclude
certain cases, such as strikes called to support workers
in other countries or taken to support fellow trade
unionists in a totally separate company. The immunity
is now restricted to disputes which occur between
employees and management in a single organization or
in an associated organization such as a different part of
the same company. It excludes 'secondary action', as
strikes called in sympathy with workers in dispute in
other companies are called.

As we saw in Chapter 1, most employees never use
their right to strike. It is the ultimate sanction, understood by both sides in negotiations to be available to the
unions as a final resort, but rarely used – although when
it is used it often attracts publicity. Without the sanction
in the background, however, the management would
have no reason to negotiate, and the union no means of
pressuring them to do so.

The legal position of a strike has in practice been of
little importance compared to the power and determination of the two sides. Few employers are willing to
prolong or exacerbate the bitterness which occurs during a strike by indulging in legal action against their
employees or their unions.

One particular issue associated with strikes arouses
much argument: picketing.

Picketing

Picketing is the act of gathering at a place of work to
persuade people to support a strike. This may involve
persuading those people to join the strike, or just to stop

deliveries to the workplace or some similar action. It creates controversy when large numbers of pickets are involved and they are considered to be intimidating. Classic examples occurred during the miners' strikes of 1972, 1974 and 1984/5, the Grunwick dispute of 1978 and the *Sunday Times* move to Wapping in 1986.

Because of the controversy, the law has changed. Picketing has been restricted by recent Acts of Parliament to the place at which the picket actually works – or, if he is a trade union official, to the place at which his members work. Much more important are the Home Secretary's advice to the police on how they handle pickets and the code of practice on picketing. Most of the obvious abuses of picketing are covered by the criminal law in any case; violence or physical intimidation is unlawful in any context.

Collective agreements

The precise nature of a contract of employment is unclear. Even the lawyers are still debating it. Important components of most individual contracts are, in practice, to be found in collective agreements, which are reached by unions and management as a result of negotiation.

The predominance of collective agreements reflects two essential facts, though there are some underlying facts which also have an impact. These two key elements are the convenience for all but the very smallest companies of having logical pay systems and arrangements, and the extensive influence of the trade unions in Britain.

Underlying facts that help us to understand the predominance of collective agreements include the power position of the parties. Individual employees are rarely able to negotiate their terms and conditions of employment in practice. They are taken on by the organization as, say, a warehouseman, on advertised pay rates. The

company may have a warehouse wage structure with
different rates depending on perhaps length of service,
or age. In any case, the employee is basically faced with
'take it or leave it'. If he is to influence the warehouseman's rate that he receives, he can only do it once
he has started work – through his union, i.e. collectively.

In most circumstances there is an insistence that the
agreements apply to all workers. On the management
side, this insistence stems from their need to maintain
the logical relationship between groups and individuals;
on the union side from their determination to avoid
non-union people being cheaper for the employer to
hire. In any one factory or office only, say, sixty per cent
of employees may be union members but the collective
agreement will apply to all employees.

Overall, the important point is that, although only
half the employees in Britain are union members, the
terms and conditions of the vast majority of employees
are determined in fact by collective agreements between
unions and management.

The legal status of this collective bargain is somewhat
unclear, however. In line with the British tradition of
voluntarism, agreements made between management
and trade unions are not legally enforceable. There was
a short period in the early 1970s when the government
of the day tried to ensure that union-management
agreements could be held by the courts to be binding on
the parties involved. But both unions and management
combined to ensure that they included in all agreements
a clause that said something to the effect that 'This Is
Not A Legally Enforceable Agreement'. (It was known,
from its initials, as a Tina Lea clause!)

It seems that, in practice, there is no half-way house.
Either you have a fully legalistic system as in the United
States of America, where agreements between unions
and managements are legal documents (often as large as

two or three books the size of this one), drawn up by lawyers acting for each side; or you have a non-legalistic system. Agreements in Britain are non-legal, drawn up often on just two or three sheets of paper by the people who have to work under them.

That seems clear enough, and yet we said two paragraphs back that the situation was unclear. What have we overlooked? The contract of employment is a contract like any other. That means it is legally enforceable. But we have just said that most contracts of employment are determined by collective agreements – and they are not legally enforceable. If you are not sure where that leaves us, do not worry: the courts are not sure either! We do know that either the individual or management can ask the courts to enforce an individual contract; we do know that the courts will not enforce a collective agreement on the unions or on management. Some elements of the collective agreement are automatically included in the individual contract – pay, for example. Other elements we just do not know about.

In practice, this uncertainty does not matter greatly. The British tradition is to resolve such issues as far as possible without recourse to the law, so that at the workplace these delicate legal problems have very little impact.

The changing face of employment law

We have seen that the passing of law is one aspect of the state's involvement in industrial relations (Chapter 4). As such it is inevitably a political and value-laden activity. In Britain, unlike many other countries, there is a continuing political debate about the part law should play in industrial relations.

Traditionally, the law stayed out of industrial relations, particularly as far as collective bargaining was concerned. Over the last few years, however, the law has become progressively more involved, providing support to union members, encouraging collective bargaining and attempting to limit the power of the unions.

The main debate centres upon how the law can improve industrial relations. One side of this debate argues that the law should provide a generally supportive framework which encourages collective bargaining, but leaves the parties concerned free to get on with it. After all, it is said, it is the managers and workforce involved who have to live with the results. Furthermore, history shows that it is difficult to enforce the law on hundreds of thousands of union members who will not accept it. History also shows that the most acrimonious disputes have been *about* the law rather than resolved by it. So, it is argued, the law should stay out.

The alternative argument is that, despite the law staying out of industrial relations, parties have not reformed themselves. Perhaps the law should be more involved in deciding who should join unions, when employers should recognize them, when they should negotiate and on what subjects, and in restricting the right to strike. The fact that such legal interventions have been less than successful in the past, or that they are contentious, is, it is argued, no reason for rejecting the good that the law can do.

6 Workplace Industrial Relations

So far we have considered what industrial relations is (in Chapter 1), looked at the main groups involved – management, unions and the state – and at the legal basis of industrial relations. But how does it all fit together? What is industrial relations like in British workplaces?

This chapter will remind you of the range of workplaces and try to place industrial relations in its day-to-day context. We will examine the social structure of work and the potential for conflict, and outline some of the formal and informal methods and procedures by which such conflicts are handled.

The variety of workplaces

The variety of work is enormous. Some people work in small offices, others in giant factories; some stay in one place, while others are constantly on the move; some jobs are clean, interesting, enjoyable; others are filthy and boring. Many people at work have a deep pride in the skill with which they perform tasks allotted to them; and there are many others for whom the task has been simplified so much that they feel like a cheap robot.

Industrial relations in context

Although, as we have pointed out, industrial relations has a continuous bearing on nearly all work situations and is constantly in the press, we need to keep it in perspective. It is not the subject of continual attention and concern in the workplace.

There will be occasions, in most workplaces, when industrial relations does come to the forefront: around the time of annual pay negotiations or in the event of a serious dispute, for example. But not only are such disputes rare in any workplace; most never experience these moments of high tension. For the majority of managers, and employees, industrial relations is a vital part of the background to their work; only occasionally, if ever, does it push its way to the front of the picture.

For some individuals, of course, industrial relations is much more than background. These are the industrial relations specialists in management, whom we considered in Chapter 2.

Industrial relations may also be a full-time preoccupation for some of the union representatives we discussed in Chapter 3: those within the work organization (the shop stewards) and the full-time officials.

The manager who is not an industrial relations specialist is in a more complicated position. Managers achieve things by or through other people. On the broader definitions at least, managers are involved in industrial relations nearly all the time – or, to be more exact, everything they are involved in has an industrial relations dimension.

Industrial relations is really an integral part of employment. From the employees' point of view, the jobs they have, the work they do and the way they are treated at work can all be seen as aspects of industrial relations. From management's point of view, their job involves motivating other people to do things, and that requires a successful industrial relations policy.

Coordination and control

For any employing organization to work effectively, there must be some form of coordination between the individuals who make up the organization, and some form of control to ensure that work is completed according to a pattern.

It is axiomatic that everyone at work in any organization has similar concerns (such as in the success of the organization). We have to recognize, however, that people will also have conflicting aspirations (such as who should be rewarded most if the organization is successful). This is the paradox of work, and the basis for our interest in industrial relations. Every organization requires coordination and control; but within every organization there are conflicting interests and arrangements must be made to accommodate them.

These arrangements are, first, the rules which are laid down in the workplace, written or unwritten, to ensure the necessary coordination and control. Second, there are procedures or steps taken to develop or enforce the rules. We will examine each in turn.

The rules

Workplace rules can be put under the following headings:

- rules made by Parliament, which we have looked at in Chapter 4
- rules made by management; important in all workplaces and especially where there is no, or only a very weak, trade union
- rules made by management and employee
- rules made by management and union; these may, of course, be applied to non-union members too. We will look at how such collective agreements are made shortly

- custom and practice; rules which, in a sense, have 'grown up' rather than been made. They are unwritten understandings about the way things are done in a workplace.

The object of these rules is to ensure coordination and control in a way that reduces to a minimum conflict about the interests of those who are being controlled. The evidence of people leaving jobs, of apathetic workers, of absenteeism and lateness, of sabotage at work and of various forms of collective industrial disputes shows that industrial conflict persists nonetheless. How widespread it is we cannot know, but it is worth stressing that in general people at work accept the rules which apply to them.

How the rules are determined and enforced varies from workplace to workplace. One pivotal factor will be whether or not a trade union, or a number of trade unions, is involved in the process. Before considering the procedures in detail, therefore, we need to establish how a union becomes recognized by an employer as having a legitimate contribution to make in a workplace.

Trade union recognition

We saw in Chapter 5 that, legally, recognition of a trade union can come through an agreement between management and union, or can be inferred from managerial actions. A series of legal rights follows, once recognition has been granted.

In practice, although there are some exceptions, unions begin to be of real benefit to their members only when they are recognized. Any degree of recognition entitles the union to the legal rights but much more important in practice is the extent of recognition. There is a range – from, at one extreme, only allowing union representatives in certain departments to accompany members during grievance or disciplinary cases to a full involvement in all major decisions made by management at the other. Typically, recognition is granted for something between these extremes. Neither the decision to recognize nor the extent of recognition is a once-and-for-all decision.

It is management which takes the decision to recognize a union. In theory, a union could claim that 100 per cent of employees were in membership and management could still refuse to recognize it. Unless management reacts positively to the involvement of a union or unions in the workplace, there is little a union can do to further its case. Obviously, the members can strike in support of that recognition claim, and each year a small proportion of the strikes recorded have been in support of recognition claims. But strike action reinforces opinions about trade unions as harmful bodies whose sole intent is to disrupt work, and it will harm establishment of the good relationship that the union is hoping to build up. So striking is a last resort.

The decision to recognize or not recognize a union lies with management.

Managers who decide to recognize unions will have weighed up such issues as the time which they will have to spend dealing with union representatives, the imposition of a structure between themselves and individual workers, and the powers which unions have to resist and modify managerial proposals. Eventually, they will have agreed to recognize the union because of one or more of the following:

- pressure from unionized employees
- pressure from outside (unionized workers in other companies that the management deals with, for example)
- a feeling that employees have a right to their own separate channel of communication
- the advantages for management of dealing with a

group or groups which represent many employees
- the advantages for management of establishing a
formal and accepted structure for handling conflict.

As we have seen, the decision to recognize can be
changed or amended.

Withdrawal of recognition already granted is not a
frequent occurrence but the extent of recognition is
more subject to change. The most usual changes are for
recognition to spread from one department or section of
the organization to another, and often from one level of
employees up the scale to their immediate superiors,
and on up into management grades. The issues bar-
gained over also tend to widen, though this is a slow
and patchy process at best. There is some evidence that
when economic circumstances of the organization
decline collective bargaining comes to focus on the
fundamentals of job protection and pay.

Decisions on recognition and extent of recognition are
key areas of management policy, and we will return to
them in the final chapter. Full recognition over an extensive range of issues can be described as a form of industrial democracy, a subject we will also discuss in more
detail in the final chapter.

The closed shop

Recognition of a trade union to represent employees
through negotiation is one thing; an insistence that all
employees should join that union is another – and a
much more controversial one. This sort of arrangement
is generally called the 'closed shop'; in law it is known
as a union membership agreement. It is one of the most
controversial issues in British industrial relations.

There are, in practice, a wide variety of closed shop
arrangements, ranging from workplaces in which all
employees are union members and in which it is

implicitly assumed that all newcomers will join, to those with very detailed written agreements between the union and management.

Like recognition, the signing of a closed shop agreement, and even the tacit acceptance of traditional 'all-union' arrangements, lies in management's hands. And in the manufacturing sector, to take one example, managements of about a third of all establishments with over fifty employees have granted closed shop arrangements.

The case against the closed shop is usually made on one or more of three grounds:

- it is based on compulsion – employees who leave the union will be sacked – and that is fundamentally unfair and undemocratic
- it can lead to injustice for individuals who do not agree with it and cannot therefore either obtain or keep a job in those workplaces
- it gives the union too much power

While there are many people in industry who would accept these points, they are made most often by people not directly involved such as politicians or newspaper leader writers. The arguments in favour of the closed shop are more often made by the unions and management involved, usually on the grounds of the existing industrial relations position:

- it ensures that those who reap the benefit of union work (all employees to whom wage increases, for example, apply) contribute to the unions; there are no 'freeloaders'
- it ensures that the union is fully representative of even the 'silent ones' who might not otherwise join
- it prevents the incursion of other unions into established arrangements: there are no non-members for them to recruit
- it ensures that disciplinary and grievance procedures are equally applicable to all employees.

The closed shop is widespread in British industry and, in practice, causes very few problems. Most closed shops exist because the vast majority of employees want them, and managements find them useful. Legislative moves to protect people from possible injustice in the arrangement have not revealed great numbers of aggrieved individuals.

Procedures

Informal arrangements

Once a union has been recognized for collective bargaining, and whether or not it has been granted a closed shop, managers and union representatives will have to establish a mechanism or range of mechanisms through which they can meet and negotiate.

In many workplaces some, at least, of the arrangements are informal and *ad hoc*. Employee representatives will be free to talk to managers about any issue at almost any time and to resolve problems over cups of coffee or in a corridor discussion. This approach has great attractions for both parties and probably operates to some degree in most workplaces where unions are recognized.

Solving the immediate problem is important, sometimes vital. The difficulties that can arise when informal, *ad hoc* approaches are favoured tend to be longer term; they result in:

- differences in the way staff are treated in different departments
- uncertainty about what the rules are
- different interpretations of the same rule
- lack of clarity about who is responsible for maintenance of certain standards
- concern on the part of those who believe they

should be responsible, but who see problems solved 'over their heads', without their involvement.

To overcome these difficulties, and under the prompting of legal requirements, most organizations employing any substantial number of people have developed formal agreements.

Formal agreement procedures

There are two main categories of agreement:

- substantive agreements – these concern the actual terms and conditions of employment, e.g. pay, hours and fringe benefits
- procedural agreements – these are concerned with the rules of negotiation. You could liken them to the Queensberry rules for boxing.

There are several types of procedural rules:

- negotiating: usually initiated by the union – decisions are reached by agreement
- redundancy: initiated by management – when they decide that the number of individuals employed must be reduced
- disciplinary (including dismissal): initiated by management – concerned with the behaviour and performance of individual employees
- grievance: initiated by the individual – deals with concerns that the individual has about the way he or she is being treated
- disputes: usually initiated by a union representative – the collective version of grievance procedures
- consultation: initiated by management – the means whereby management informs employees of a problem and takes their views into account before reaching a decision.

The procedures take the form of a series of steps. If an

issue is not resolved at one step, it will be taken on to consideration by more senior people on each side at the next step.

For procedures to be effective, they need to be credible. Employees need to regard them as reasonably fair and not as a device for delaying settlements for as long as possible. The advantages to management of good procedures can easily be underestimated. Among these advantages are that the various management representatives feel more confident in knowing just what the decision-making procedure is and the precise part they play in it. Experienced negotiators can use procedures to define clearly what the problems are and, if they are not resolved, at least to agree what the points of difference are and who takes the next step. Emotional heat associated with disputes can lead to many misperceptions of the real issues; good procedures, skilfully used, can do much to avoid unnecessary misunderstanding.

The development of joint procedures can make dealing with employees and unions very much easier, but procedures do not exist in a vacuum. However good a procedure is it cannot compensate for inefficient working arrangements.

Some workplaces – civil service offices are a good example – have very detailed negotiating arrangements, staff up to very high levels, including many managers, in union membership and a long tradition of dealing with all major problems at work through a process of consultation and negotiation. In some workplaces, issues such as pay and conditions are negotiated while other subjects, such as changing work organization, are left to management. This can happen in a retail store, for example. Engineering companies often have elaborate arrangements for shop stewards and staff representatives to meet frequently to 'filter' issues raised by their members and to put the more serious ones 'into procedure'.

Workplaces vary, not only in arrangements for meeting to resolve conflicts of interest, but also in who is involved. On the management side it might be certain levels of management at different steps; personnel or industrial relations specialists may or may not be included. On the union side, it might be the individual alone, the employee representative or the full-time official. Some organizations have what is known as an 'external' stage at the end of their procedures. Here, unresolved issues are sent outside the workplace for employers' associations and trade union confederation officials to resolve, or a conciliator or arbitrator is appointed from outside both management and union.

The individual procedures

More common than collective procedures, and applicable to all employing organizations, are the individual procedures: grievance and discipline.

Handling grievances. When the relationship between employee and company is proving unsatisfactory to the employee, then he or she is said to have a grievance. A grievance might be about an individual's pay or the kind of work they are asked to do.

When an employee has such a grievance, there are many ways in which it can be expressed. If it is serious enough, the employee might leave the organization; this happens hundreds of thousands of times a year. But leaving a job is a hard choice, particularly if the employee is well paid, has a senior position or has been with the organization a long time – and particularly given the present levels of unemployment. So many employees with a grievance will continue at their job.

The alternative to a thorough grievance procedure and to a management style which encourages people to raise their grievances is that unhappy or discontented employees complain to the wrong people, spread dissatisfaction, work without enthusiasm or perhaps act destructively.

It is to management's advantage if the grievance is expressed through a formal, accepted procedure so that it can be dealt with properly. This may mean correcting some information the employee has misinterpreted; it may be the opportunity to put right something that has gone wrong in the work or in relationships between individuals. Sometimes just airing the grievance is enough. Even if the problem cannot be resolved, it nearly always helps if the employee can see that it has been taken seriously and the concerns understood.

Procedures for raising and handling grievances have developed within the British tradition of voluntarism. They are agreements about the way issues will be dealt with, but they are not legally binding.

Table 5 (p.99) is a copy of a procedure in operation today. The main points to note are:

- the first step in nearly all grievance procedures is for employees to raise the issue with their immediate boss
- the levels of management and, where appropriate, union involvement are clearly stated at every stage
- the procedures stress resolution of issues as soon as possible. Some procedures put time limits on every stage to emphasize the point
- this procedure has an external stage where 'third party' conciliation or arbitration is used when the two main parties (management and union) fail to agree
- this company has an 'open door' policy so that any individual can talk to a senior manager, at any time. Other companies would argue that this leads to individuals 'bypassing' the procedure and they would not allow it.

The right of any employee, whether a trade union member or not, to request a personal interview with his department head shall be in no way limited by this procedure. It is accepted by all parties to this agreement that the most satisfactory solution to a problem results when agreement is reached between the individual and his superiors. The procedure for handling requests or complaints is for use in the event of the parties being unable to agree. Every attempt will be made to deal with grievances as soon as possible. If the union representatives feel there has been unnecessary delay, the industrial relations manager and union official will investigate the complaint. The stages in the procedure will be:

Stage 1
The employee having a request or complaint arising from his employment will raise the matter with his appropriate superior and, together with him, every effort will be made to resolve the problem. Failing settlement, the employee will proceed to the next stage.

Stage 2
The employee and his local representative, if requested, will meet the employee's manager. Failing settlement, the matter will be referred to the appropriate senior managers or their deputies. A report of the proceedings will then be submitted to the industrial relations manager and, where applicable, to the full-time official of the union.

Stage 3
Without undue delay, a meeting will be arranged between the individual concerned, the trade union's full-time official, the local representative, the industrial relations manager and the appropriate management representative.

Stage 4

Failing settlement at Stage 3, the matter may be referred by either party to the Advisory, Conciliation and Arbitration Service for conciliation; or by mutual agreement the company and the trade union can be taken to independent arbitration through the Advisory, Conciliation and Arbitration Service. In this event the decision of the arbitrator(s) will be final and binding on both parties.

Table 5 *Example of an individual grievance procedure*

A rough-and-ready '90 per cent rule' seems to apply in almost every workplace. That is, 90 per cent (more or less) of grievances are satisfactorily resolved at the initial discussion with the supervisor. Of those which go into formal procedure, 90 per cent (more or less) are resolved at the first stage; of those that are not, 90 per cent are satisfactorily concluded at the second stage, and so on.

Handling disciplinary cases. Grievances occur when the relationship between employee and organization is proving unsatisfactory to the employee. When the relationship is proving unsatisfactory to the management, there may be a case for disciplinary action.

Just as grievances may be resolved constructively in all sorts of ways, with procedures as only one possibility, so may disputes about the employee's behaviour or performance. The employee may be dismissed and a replacement hired – usually a time-consuming and expensive process. Poor behaviour or inadequate performance may be tolerated, with much private moaning by the managers concerned. This happens frequently. Sometimes the employees (and the problems) are transferred to another department.

There are more positive approaches: carefully

designed training, a new challenge or the use of appropriate disciplinary procedures.

Dictionary definitions of discipline contain the following elements.

'Discipline' (as a noun):

- instruction
- branch of learning, or field of study
- training
- mode of life in accordance with rules
- subjection to control
- order
- severe training
- mortification
- punishment
- instrument of penance or punishment.

'To discipline' (as a verb):

- to subject to discipline
- to train
- to educate
- to bring under control
- to chastise.

It is interesting how far down the list is the idea of discipline as punishment, though this is still a common view of discipline in many work organizations. The current accepted wisdom is that discipline should be seen as a corrective and preventive measure, putting the employee back on the right path, rather than as a punishment for going wrong. The corrective approach is both more humanitarian and more cost-effective, but we do not know how many managers actually use discipline this way in practice. In theory it is clear that the aim of disciplinary action is to ensure that the breach of standards is not repeated either by the individual (or group) being disciplined or by others.

Table 6 outlines some of the main advice given in

disciplinary procedures in the code of practice. Table 7 gives some practical advice on the way disciplinary cases should be handled.

Disciplinary procedures should:

(a) Be in writing
(b) Specify to whom they apply
(c) Provide for matters to be dealt with quickly
(d) Indicate the disciplinary actions which may be taken
(e) Specify the levels of management which have authority to take the various forms of disciplinary action, ensuring that immediate superiors do not normally have the power to dismiss without reference to senior mangement
(f) Provide for individuals to be informed of the complaints against them and to be given an opportunity to state their case before decisions are reached
(g) Give individuals the right to be accompanied by a trade union representative or by a fellow employee of their choice
(h) Ensure that, except for gross misconduct, no employees are dismissed for a first breach of discipline
(i) Ensure that disciplinary action is not taken until the case has been carefully investigated
(j) Provide a right of appeal and specify the procedure to be followed.

Table 6 *Code of practice advice on disciplinary procedures*

1 Gather together the facts, including precise details of the standards that should have been reached; ensure that there really is a problem and decide what standard the employee should be achieving.

2 Consider whether there was a written rule, and whether the rule has been enforced. Did the employee know about the rule?

3 Give the employee a chance to give his side of the story, in private. Encourage a two-way conversation; consider the employee's replies and, if necessary, adjourn the meeting while any new facts are considered.

4 Check on the company's own procedure to see what the next appropriate stage is if you are not satisfied with the employee's replies; should you be giving an informal, formal, oral or written warning?

5 Whatever disciplinary action is taken, ensure first that it is appropriate and that 'the punishment fits the crime'. Ensure that the employee understands why you are taking the action.

6 Consider what effect action will have on other employees.

7 Ensure that written warnings detail, in specific terms wherever possible, what improvements are expected, within what period of time, and the consequences if the improvement is not made, is insufficient or is not maintained.

8 Monitor the employee's behaviour following the disciplinary action.

Table 7 *Advice on handling disciplinary cases*

Non-union methods

In addition to arrangements agreed with or involving the trade unions, there are methods of resolving disputes of interest at work which do not include the unions. Some of these are found in organizations which recognize trade unions as well as those which do not; others are found only in non-union firms.

In the first category – methods which do not include the union but are found in unionized as well as non-union firms – we can include:

- a range of management controls
- a series of information-passing and consultative arrangements
- informal relationships.

Management controls operate in every organization and, even in the most participative, only a few are the subject of collective bargaining. It is most unusual, for example, for unions to influence a department's budget or financial targets for the year. However, these may be very important in industrial relations; they can make some solutions to problems possible, others almost impossible. Other conflicts of interest may be obscured or resolved through a performance appraisal system or a work reorganization or through retraining. Only in a minority of cases are unions involved in such decisions.

Consultative arrangements and methods of passing information up and down the organization are rarely limited to a union-only channel. Consultative meetings, such as safety committees, shop councils, social committees and progress review groups, all perform a valuable function in helping individuals and managers to cope with differing interests as well as in achieving their ostensible aims. And a vast amount of money is being spent yearly on purchasing the knowledge of consultants who can advise on 'briefing groups', 'quality circles' or whatever the latest fashion in passing information may be. These are all channels to which unions have no formal access.

Informal relationships are, in many ways, the most important means of resolving different interests. It is in the nature of management that much of a manager's task includes the informal coaxing, cajoling, 'jollying along' of subordinates that is almost indistinguishable from social conversation. The most effective line managers are often those most skilled at developing and using these informal methods. This is an aspect of manage-ment that is far from the high-powered jet-set, executive image that is sometimes portrayed. But this unglamor-ous aspect of the job is perhaps the part where most potential conflicts of interest between managers and employees are handled and prevented from becoming serious disputes.

Summary

We have seen then that the freedom which British employment law grants to the parties in industrial rela-tions and the wide variety of managements and trade unions have led to tremendous diversity of practice at the workplace. No two workplaces are alike. No two workplaces have the same industrial relations.

In very few workplaces is industrial relations a central preoccupation. Rather, the conflicting interests of management and employees are handled in various ways, only some of which come within the usual defini-tions of industrial relations. In workplaces where unions are recognized there are, in addition to collective procedures developed specifically to regulate the rel-tionship between managers and unions, individual grievance and disciplinary procedures. Even in the most highly unionized companies, however, informal arrangements play an important part in workplace industrial relations.

7 Management Policies

It has been a theme throughout this book that of the three main parties to industrial relations – management, unions and the state – it is management which carries major responsibility for developing and maintaining industrial relations at the workplace. We conclude with a consideration of managerial policies in industrial relations, to see what it is that managements are, or could be, trying to achieve and how they are, or how they could be, planning to meet those objectives.

Trends

In societies such as Britain where economic growth is no longer virtually automatic (and that includes most societies now), a key problem can be summed up in the word 'performance'.

At national, company and individual level, technical capability is expanding enormously. We have access to sophisticated machinery, robotics and computers to enable small groups of individuals to produce the goods or provide the services which it took thousands of people to produce or provide only a few years ago. Even where jobs have not changed all that much in terms of technology, our ability to organize work more rationally and our more sophisticated training techniques have had an impact on what can be achieved.

Increasingly, however, the problem is becoming what people are prepared to do. They are no longer so prepared to work hard for ten or twelve hours a day, six days a week, fifty or fifty-one weeks a year.

People now have rising expectations about the conditions they will work in, how clean they are, how socially enjoyable. They have expectations about the way they are treated in terms of material reward; and also in terms of status and respect. And they have ideas about how they would like to see the work organized, the product or service sold, and the results invested.

Managing industrial relations

Increased technology in a post-industrial society puts more power in the hands of the man or woman who controls the computer; and in troubled economies it is more important to manage employees properly so that their hopes and concerns are met and they are motivated to perform effectively. So, paradoxically, industrial relations, at least on a wider definition, becomes more not less important.

In future years, industrial relations will continue to be important because:

- for the state, efficiently managed staff, a lack of industrial disruption and a constructive relationship with trade unions will be central to economic improvement
- for employees and their unions, employment, and the way people are treated at work, will be vital to their well-being
- for management, good industrial relations, and the policies to bring them about, will be prerequisites for success.

Industrial relations policies

An industrial relations policy is 'a set of proposals and actions that act as a reference point for managers in their dealings with employees'. This is wider than some other definitions, which assume a policy has to be written down. Our definition implies that all organizations will have some form of policy because, in most organizations, managers and other employees can establish what the senior executives will tolerate or encourage in the treatment of staff. In some companies, 'cowboy' building or road haulage firms for example, the policy amounts to no more than a general understanding that they will do whatever they can get away with provided it brings in the cash.

'Espoused' policy and 'operational' policy

We can distinguish two forms of policy. One is the more narrowly defined industrial relations policy formalized in managerial statements and documents which outline sets of principles or procedures. This is the 'espoused' policy. It explains what management would like to achieve in its industrial relations if possible.

Managers are sometimes guided in their actions by espoused policies. Their problem is, however, that the subject of industrial relations for the line manager is only rarely identifiable as a separate topic. In most cases, it is bound up with day-to-day running of the workplace. The way staff are treated is much more closely related to the way work is organized and carried out than it is to an espoused industrial relations policy. Managers organize work according to the pressures and priorities placed on them by senior management in the form of demands for some type of output from the manager's section – products or services. These pressures and the priorities they indicate lead the managers to act in certain ways and avoid acting in others. Because such pressures and priorities are also controlled by senior management we can describe these too as a policy: the 'operational' policy.

In practice, managers try to follow the operational policy: to do what it is that senior managers want them to do, taking account of all priorities and problems. Managers down the line will follow espoused industrial relations policy only where it is part of the operational policy.

In general in this chapter we talk not about the broad statements of principle which managements sometimes issue, but rather about operational policy. We are less concerned with whether management has issued a document stating that it will consult with shop stewards, for example, than with whether arrangements are made and managers checked to ensure that such consultations take place. Our concern is with the practical way senior executives indicate, by word and deed, that some things are required from line managers, whilst others would merely be good provided that they did not interfere with more important matters like production, sales or customer service. It is, after all, this operational policy which determines the way managers behave.

Industrial relations objectives

We can summarize what management is aiming for in its industrial relations policies under the following general headings:

- simplicity
- control
- stability and predictability
- efficiency.

Only a few years ago, we might have included as one objective industrial peace or the absence of conflict. That will certainly remain a key objective for most managements. But it is less central to modern policies because managers are coming to see that the policy of peace-at-any-price is shortsighted. The other objectives outlined are more important and, sometimes, worth the risk of disruption.

We could also have included in the list some idea of fairness or justice, and some requirement to abide by the law. These are principles all managements need to set out in any written policy and they are criteria most managers try to follow. In the operational policy, however, these will be *methods* to achieve the sort of objectives we have indicated above, rather than objectives in themselves.

Simplicity

The objective of simplicity has developed partly in response to the complexities and associated problems of industrial relations which are all too evident in many companies. Managements are faced with a multiplicity of unions, often antagonistic to each other, and a multiplicity of bargaining arrangements, leading to a highly varied and complex wage structure. Management policies aim to simplify these arrangements.

The simplest arrangement is where management negotiates one annual wage increase with one union which covers all members of staff. 'Single union' agreements have attracted much press attention but are, in reality, unobtainable in many British workplaces. The complexity of union arrangements has been overcome in the past by developing joint union arrangements within the workplace, or by creating a variety of different bargaining units. These approaches remain, but organizations are increasingly considering alternative approaches.

Managements generally aim to reduce the number of bargaining units to as few as possible. Bargaining units – the different groups with which managements negotiate – can be simplified by amalgamation so that fewer negotiations take place, or by reducing the number of unions within each group. The first option is, to some extent, under managerial control; they are one of the parties to the negotiations. The second option is not; but managers can have some influence on the strength of particular unions.

Managers can influence the success of particular unions. They can develop strategies allowing one union in an area to achieve 'victories' handling grievance or disciplinary cases; they can be seen to treat one union with more respect, involving it more than another. These are long-term strategies, but they can be successful in restricting the appeal of trade unions in one area to a particular union that managers are trying to encourage. Greater simplicity carries several benefits for managements:

- saving of managerial time (one or two sets of negotiations rather than seven or eight)
- removal of barriers between groups (hence making it easier for employees to accept moves from one group to another and increase the flexible and efficient use of manpower).

Control

A central aim of many managerial policies in industrial relations is control of manpower.

Control outside employment is already commonplace in some areas. Certain services are traditionally performed by employees of other organizations, or by self-employed people. Window-cleaning and accountancy, secretarial 'temps' and security services are typical examples. Local authorities often 'contract out' tasks, such as refuse collection, that have traditionally been performed by council employees – and many private companies do likewise. Control of the contract is by price and service; control of staff is delegated, as it were, to the contractor.

Within the workplace, control operates very differently. We have looked at disciplinary rules and procedures. More supervisors are being trained to operate such procedures effectively. Indeed, supervisory and management training is expanding generally.

Disciplinary procedures are only one form of control which management can adopt. Some controls are built in to budgetary systems or to machinery. If a production line moves at a particular speed, that will itself control how fast the employees there work; management has to do little to control at least the speed of their work. Similarly, new computerized programmes allow managers to see very easily how much work their subordinates are doing, and how effective that work is. Other controls exist in performance targets, in monthly and quarterly reports on the work of the department or in annual performance appraisals.

Of course, all controls by management may be opposed by employees who belong to trade unions. When levels of unemployment are high the unions' power may be muted. Some managements use such an opportunity to establish or re-establish control over employees in an aggressive way. More sophisticated managements establish which controls are most appropriate for them and ensure they operate effectively and do not create antipathy in the workforce.

Stability and predictability

A third industrial relations objective for managers is stability. The fewer unplanned occurrences the better. Good management tries therefore to establish and maintain systems and procedures to handle conflict effectively and without disruption of work.

Stability should not be confused with absence of conflict or lack of change. The first is not feasible in an industrial society; the problem is not existence of conflict but whether it can be handled effectively and used constructively. A lack of change should worry any management. Organizations which remain static in a rapidly changing environment will soon become outmoded. If industrial relations arrangements within the organization are effective, they will facilitate change without compounding the difficulties by being continually in flux themselves.

Communications systems can usually be improved. Managers try to ensure that clear messages and information are passed down the hierarchy to non-managerial employees. They try to be as receptive as possible to the concerns and grievances of their staff. Supervisors should assess morale and try to deal with small issues before they become major problems.

Those organizations which have developed coherent strategies attempt to ensure that more important issues are directed through established channels. Detailed grievance procedures are developed, with the trade unions where appropriate, so that employees have access to a formalized and accepted method of resolving issues. For issues that involve groups, the organization may have a separate 'disputes procedure'.

More extensive information passing, both up and down the organization, and more detailed and elaborate grievance/disputes procedures, will give managements more warning of conflict. A more formal link between negotiating groups is also desirable, within and outside the organization, so that the danger of 'leapfrogging' – each group alternately jumping above the other in wage or salary terms – is reduced.

These factors contribute towards the linked objective of 'predictability'. One obvious way of increasing predictability is to extend the period of agreements. The declining rate of inflation during the mid 1980s led to a trend in this direction; when employees are confident that the value of money will not decrease too much over a longer period, they are prepared to accept longer-term agreements. Pay deals that last for two or even three years are common in some countries already; they are becoming more widespread in the United Kingdom.

Increasing predictability in industrial relations enables managers to plan ahead, directing and coordinating human resources within the organization in much the same way that they do with resources such as cash or machinery.

Efficiency

There are definitional problems when we use a term such as 'efficiency' in relation to manpower. The efficiency of an engine or a computer can be agreed and measured; we can measure certain factors in manpower, but not others. And there is often disagreement about the criteria we should adopt. Take an example. Warehousemen empty and stack lorries as they arrive at the warehouse. Suppose, through scheduling or traffic difficulties, no lorries arrive during the afternoon, then several arrive together, entailing overtime by the warehousemen. Has their efficiency gone down? (Manpower costs to unload the same number of lorries have increased.) Should the men be asked to do something else whilst waiting for the lorry? What could they do that would leave them free to start unloading as soon as a lorry arrived?

Efficiency, in a manpower context, has two components: keeping costs as low as possible, and increasing output. Keeping costs down traditionally involves employing no more people than necessary to do the job and employing them as cheaply as possible. It is now understood that this is too narrow a view of costs. Keeping numbers as low as possible, for instance, may mean that big new contracts have to be passed up, because the organization is not geared to cope with them. And employing staff as cheaply as possible may mean that the organization has poor quality staff, with little training, no enthusiasm to do the job properly and little commitment to present management.

Sensible managements, therefore, try to establish, through manpower planning systems, what numbers and what kind of manpower they will need, and what they will have to offer to attract such manpower. Keeping costs to a minimum will remain an aim but will be subordinated to other objectives. This involves a sharper, more hard-headed look at manpower costs than traditional 'hire 'em when it's good: fire 'em when it's bad' approaches and can lead to a different wage and benefit package or structure, and sometimes to higher pay for individuals working in these organizations.

The trend is thus for a reduction in costs, but set in the context of rigorous examination of manpower requirements. On the output side, managements try to:

- increase labour flexibility
- increase commitment
- extend the range of bargaining.

Labour flexibility Four types of restrictions reduce management's ability to use any employee in any appropriate task:

- restrictions imposed by law
- restrictions arising from lack of capability to do particular tasks
- restrictions arising from managerially determined divisions within the workforce ('division of labour')
- restrictions arising from employee determined divisions within the workforce ('demarcation').

These categories overlap but they help us to understand

the types of restriction on labour flexibility and how an industrial relations policy can help to cope with them.

Legal restrictions on flexibility are, as we have seen, very limited. There are some restrictions on work by young persons, pilots, drivers, etc., but, in general, the law stays out of this area.

Lack of capability is perhaps the major limitation on management's use of labour. If individuals simply cannot do a task, they cannot be used for it. Managements are developing policies to resolve this problem. They organize new training and retraining initiatives. In the past, people often remained in the same specialism throughout their working lives. Nowadays people may have half a dozen or more different types of job during a working life.

An individual employee is also restricted in what he can achieve, in his efficiency, by the technology at his disposal. The pace of technological change is advancing rapidly. New technology throws into question the efficiency of all established working practices.

Division of labour, the splitting of tasks between individuals, is one of the main features of a developed economy. The idea of division of labour is central to all ideas of scientific management. Many divisions within the workforce, and the development of barriers which it is difficult to cross, have been instigated by management.

Breaking down some, at least, of these barriers is a key to successful industrial relations policies. The pace of change is so fast that what seemed formerly to be sensible divisions are now inhibiting progress. They do not look so sensible. Divisions between manual and non-manual workers become a problem when manual workers have to programme computer-aided machinery, or when managers want clerical employees to do overtime for which they have not traditionally been paid. Many companies adopt policies of 'harmonization' – establishing identical conditions of employment (other than salary, and some service-related privileges) for all employees. This has the dual benefit of (1) being seen to be fair and (2) promoting flexibility: there are fewer financial reasons why an employee should not switch from one task to another.

Demarcation problems arise when employees decide that a particular individual or group, and only that individual or group, should perform a particular task.

It has been a feature of industrial relations policies in many organizations to negotiate out such demarcation lines. This is difficult while other divisions continue. Today's division of labour is often tomorrow's demarcation dispute. Increasingly, private sector organizations are moving towards the 'single status' position of the civil service or some Japanese companies, where boundaries are reduced to a minimum so that employees are available and prepared to move from one task to another.

Commonly quoted advantages for employees of having a flexible workforce are:

- it is fairer if everyone's treatment is the same
- it makes work more interesting if you can do something different now and again
- it may mean that your company can compete better, and thus your job is more secure
- it enables employees to develop their abilities and skills.

Increasing commitment There are very few workplaces where a manager could rely on 'dumb obedience'. The best way to sabotage almost any organization is to obey orders to the letter: no more and no less. In practice, organizations rely on a measure of interest, enthusiasm and creativity on the part of their employees. As technology advances, jobs are likely to become more complex, or more boring – or both! Managers need to develop industrial relations policies such that people want to work; they have to generate motivation and commitment.

Various approaches include:

- increased participation in decision-making
- increased information about the organization and its performance
- sabbaticals: time off to study or 'recharge the batteries' in some other way
- fairer disciplinary handling
- salary-linked or other incentives for good performance.

Extending the bargaining range Traditionally, it has been the unions which have argued for an extension in the range of bargaining, and management which has fought to restrict it. This may be changing. Unions are increasingly concerned to concentrate on job security and wages. It is now managers who put new factors into that debate: persuading trade unions to negotiate on quality control, on disciplinary standards or on distribution of incentives.

Extending the issues which are negotiated in this way has the benefit to management of bringing the 'output' side of the contract of employment into focus and avoiding a complete focus on the 'costs' side. It also commits the union representatives involved in the negotiation (morally at least) to ensure that quality is maintained, or discipline improved or whatever other change is agreed. Bargaining about employees' output is still uncommon, but may become more widespread.

Developing the policies

These objectives – simplicity, control, stability, predictability and efficiency – are crucial aspects of managerial industrial relations policies.

But while the objectives we have considered so far in this chapter are generally held by all organizations, no two will apply them in the same manner. For a small company in an expanding and competitive market, the needs of efficiency may well be paramount and management will be prepared to forgo other objectives to some extent. For a large bureaucracy, the objectives of simplicity and control may carry most weight. Not only will the balance of these objectives vary, the way each objective is translated into an operational policy will be different. A management consultancy might rely heavily on a policy linking pay clearly to income generated; such a policy would be simple, relatively under control and stable, and apparently does much to motivate consultants. Such an approach would not be feasible in a social services department.

Exactly how policies are developed also varies. In many companies, including many in the public sector, industrial relations policies are at present assumed to be the preserve of industrial relations specialists.

The problems implicit in giving responsibility for industrial relations policies to specialists include:

- specialists may be somewhat divorced from day-to-day management of staff; so the policy may be inappropriate as a guideline for managers.
- specialists may not have access to the top decision-makers; so the policy may remain an espoused policy rather than become operational
- specialists may have different understandings of policies that the organization has in other areas; so may develop industrial relations policies that conflict with, say, financial or customer-service policies
- specialists may not have authority to enforce aspects of the policy on line managers; so the policy will lose credibility.

Many companies have elevated industrial relations

specialists to the board of directors, thus putting them among the power holders and increasing their authority. Other companies have moved in the opposite direction, reducing personnel or industrial relations departments and putting more responsibility for this area on to line managers.

Many organizations still regard all manpower issues as a nuisance – detailed and annoying intrusions which have to be faced once the important decisions have been made, when management is trying to implement those decisions. Many companies appreciate, however, that industrial relations is important in a positive sense. Managers in such organizations treat industrial relations as a specialism in its own right, employing experts to create progressive espoused industrial relations policies. Some bigger companies are moving away from detailed, clearly written policy documents as a focus of activities towards a more generalized understanding among senior executives of the need to integrate man management into all other aspects of the business.

Further Reading

There are a lot of detailed areas of industrial relations which it has not been possible to cover in this succinct management guide to the subject. If you wish to know more you may want to read further books, journals or articles.

Books

There are a number of good general text-books available:

H. Clegg, *The Changing System of Industrial Relations in Great Britain*, Blackwell, 1979.
The standard academic text.

R. Hyman, *Industrial Relations, A Marxist Introduction*, Macmillan, 1975.
For an alternative, still somewhat academic, approach.

G. S. Bain (Ed), *Industrial Relations in Britain*, Blackwell, 1983.
One of the best recent guides to industrial relations, with chapters by some distinguished academics.

G. Palmer, *British Industrial Relations*, Allen and Unwin, 1983.
A straightforward, well-written, overall summary; already a standard course book.

T. Keenoy, *Invitation to Industrial Relations*, Blackwell, 1985.
An interesting and thought-provoking new introductory text.

The two best books to read on the managerial side of industrial relations are:

C. J. Brewster and S. L. Connock, *Industrial Relations: Cost Effective Strategies*, Hutchinson, 1985.
An innovative attempt to summarize new developments in the current industrial relations scene.

M. Marchington, *Managing Industrial Relations*, McGraw-Hill, 1982.
A good, straightforward text.

There are very many more books on the union side of industrial relations than there are on management. The best two to read might be:

K. Coats and T. Topham, *Trade Unions in Britain*, Spokesman Books, 1983.
Outlines all the major issues and provides a sensible understanding of what the unions are and what they do.

J. Eaton and C. G. Gill, *The Trade Union Directory: A Guide to all TUC Unions*, Pluto Press, 1983.
Details each of the trade unions in the TUC with current organization, names and background. Very useful if you want to know more about a particular union (though getting rather out of date).

For a more detailed understanding of industrial relations at the workplace, though unfortunately still concentrating on the declining manufacturing sector, the best two books are:

W. Brown, *The Changing Contours of British Industrial Relations*, Blackwell, 1981.
A good statistically-based guide to what's happening in manufacturing.

E. Batstone, *Working Order*, Blackwell, 1983.
Summarizes, on the basis of a detailed statistical survey, changes in workplace industrial relations in manufacturing.

All of these books contain further references again if you get deeply involved in industrial relations as a subject.

Journals

The Employment Gazette, published by the Department of Employment, is invaluable. Other journals devoted to industrial relations include *Industrial Relations Review and Report* and *Incomes Data Services*, both available on direct subscription; and *Personnel Management*, the Institute of Personnel Management's magazine. There is also *Employee Relations*.

More academic journals are also available. The most relevant are the *British Journal of Industrial Relations* and the *Industrial Relations Journal*.

Other

You should not overlook the often free publications available from official bodies. ACAS issues guides and Codes of Practice; the Department of Employment has many guides to legislation and Codes of Practice available; and other bodies such as the Health and Safety Executive, the Equal Opportunities Commission and the Commission for Racial Equality have a lot of material they will send you.

You can also learn much about industrial relations by watching television, listening to the radio and reading newspapers. Remember always that we are dealing with a value-laden and emotive subject. The best place to read about industrial relations is in the labour column of the *Financial Times*.

Index

Index

Reference and information

☐ **North-South**	Brandt Commission	£2.50p
☐ **The Multilingual Business Handbook**	P. Hartley et al.	£3.95p
☐ **Militant Islam**	Godfrey Jansen	£1.50p
☐ **Dictionary of British History**	John Kenyon	£3.50p
☐ **How to Study**	H. Maddox	£1.95p
☐ **A Guide to Saving and Investment**	James Rowlatt	£2.95p
☐ **Career Choice**	Audrey Segal	£3.95p
☐ **Logic and its Limits**	Patrick Shaw	£2.95p
☐ **Straight and Crooked Thinking**	R. H. Thouless	£1.95p
☐ **The New Fascists**	Paul Wilkinson	£2.50p
☐ **A Dictionary of Astronomy**		£2.95p
☐ **Dictionary of Physical Sciences**		£2.95p
☐ **Dictionary of Political Thought**		£3.95p
☐ **Pan Dictionary of Synonyms and Antonyms**		£2.50p

All these books are available at your local bookshop or newsagent, or can be ordered direct from the publisher. Indicate the number of copies required and fill in the form below   12

....

Name_____
(Block letters please)

Address_____

_____

Send to CS Department, Pan Books Ltd, PO Box 40, Basingstoke, Hants
Please enclose remittance to the value of the cover price plus:
35p for the first book plus 15p per copy for each additional book ordered
to a maximum charge of £1.25 to cover postage and packing
Applicable only in the UK

While every effort is made to keep prices low, it is sometimes
necessary to increase prices at short notice. Pan Books reserve
the right to show on covers and charge new retail prices which
may differ from those advertised in the text or elsewhere